Latin Synonyms

Defined From Two Standpoints,

(1) **From the Historical and Derivative;**

(2) **From the Natural and Logical**

 As from the presence of the following Intrinsic and Undeniable Concepts:

(a) **Generic and Specific Ideas,**

(b) **Primary and Secondary Ideas,**

(c) **Dynamic and Static Ideas,**

(d) **Measure and Thing to be Measured.**

———————BY——— ---

ROBT. WM. DOUTHAT, PH. D.,

Prof. of the Latin Language and Literature
in the West Virginia University,
Morgantown, W. Va.

PREFACE

The need of some explanation of the real differences in the use and meanings of words is found to be necessary from the very beginning of our course of study in a foreign language. Otherwise, the ordinary student of a foreign tongue will make as many blunders as the Frenchman who had concluded from a short stay in this country that living in America was very "COSTIVE," and that, if he could once get hold of all the ways in which "GOT" is used, he would know two-thirds of the English language.

Students of Latin will sometimes try to translate an Eng. sentence by the first words they find answering to the Eng. words. For example, the following sentence is given in English to be turned into Latin:—"The whole farm *is covered* with sheep and cattle and hogs and chickens." The student finds TEGO means "*to cover*" and writes TEGITUR and then the sentence to a Roman would mean "the whole farm "*is roofed in*" with sheep and cattle and hogs and chickens," so that the rains cannot get to the land any more and the earth will keep dry. In other words, hogs and cattle and sheep and chickens are spread so thick over a raised platform that neither rain or sunshine can reach the ground underneath. Again, "*the dialogue is made to rest* on the authority of men of the olden times." FACERE means '*to make*' and REQUIESCERE means '*to rest.*' Then the student writes REQUIESCERE FACTUS EST, which to the Roman mind meant '*is made to go to sleep.*'

Take the expression in Eng.. '*a good deal*,' and dictate to a student "he had a good deal in his basket," pronouncing carelessly the word '*deal*,' as many do, making it 'EAL. The student will soon speak out,— "teacher, I know all the words in that sentence perfectly well, except EEL. Will you please tell me what that is in Latin?"

Take the expression "*bellied sails*" or "*full sails;*" you would not look for the VENTREFACTA VELA or VELA ALVEATA or VELA PLENA, but for VELA PASSA, '*spread sails.*'

Take such an expression as "*full day*"; you would not use PLENUS nor COMPLETUS, but SOLIDUS, INTEGER, or TOTUS.

What the student wants is a clear conception of the true meaning of a word, and then he will be able to understand the writer or to express himself with exactness and force; but, if he does not know the difference in the use of synonyms, he will blunder in his thinking and also in his expression.

Now, we may sometimes think that the student is the only one at fault in this matter. He has studied carelessly, has not been critical, etc.. etc. But the truth of the matter is the fact that NINE-TENTHS of those who have studied Latin or Greek for *three* or *five* years, and who know the grammatical relations of words well, do not know the differences of words, which, having the same meanings in the vocabularies, carry immense differences in their values. And now comes the astonishing feature in the case, viz., that fully ONE-HALF of the TEACHERS OF LATIN do not know and therefore cannot explain these differences, and at least ONE-HALF of the OTHER HALF will depend on *vague* and *unsatisfactory* definitions and have absolutely no principle of interpretation. Put up for examination the 50,000 TEACHERS of Latin in the United States and let the examination be wholly on synonyms. THREE-FOURTHS, or 37.500 will not grade 50 out of 100, and 25,000 will not grade 25 out of 100, and 10,000 will not grade 10 out of 100, and yet, to get the true value of a translation from Latin into English depends as much on the *exact rendering* of a verb or a noun or an adjective or adverb or a preposition as it does on *cases* or *modes and tenses*. No rendering by simple mode and tense or case can ever satisfy a critical mind. The true meaning of the word must be known, and this cannot be known, unless the difference between any two words with similar meanings is clear,—clear by definitions, clear by some principle of interpretation, or clear by the historical and derivative connection of the word.

We feel therefore that, next to Grammar, there must be a clearing up of the differences existing among synonymous words, and this constitutes our apology for making this book along lines already definitely drawn.

And now a word to my fellow teachers as to the method to be pursued in the use of the book.

(1) No student, much less teacher, would ever stultify himself by saying that there are not GENERAL and SPECIFIC terms employed by the Latin; for, if we go no further, all *Neuters are generic.* When Cæsar said *pugnandum est.* he meant that *everybody fought.* We know also that RES is the most *generic term* among nouns, meaning *anything visible* or *invi ible, anything that can be imagined* or *dreamed of as an object or subject..* Then for all actions, AGERE is the most generic term among verbs, etc., etc.

The difference between GENERICS and SPECIFICS should be pointed out frequently and made clear to the comprehension of every student, at least after he has had his first year in the study of the *forms* of *Nouns, Verbs, Adjectives,* etc.

(2) PRIMARY and SECONDARY words should also have attention, but these might be left for the *Third Year,* as these require a higher degree of intelligence and wider range of thought than do the *General* and *Special,* and yet the *Primary* and *Secondary* are equally as important as the *Generic* and *Specific.* As examples of the *Primary* and *Secondary,* most of the *Prepositions* are *primary,* but DE is certainly *secondary* and 1001 things may be explained from its *secondary meaning* that could not be so well explained in any other way.

(3) DYNAMIC and STATIC ideas require a still wider reach of thought and therefore should not have much attention before the *fourth year of the course.* but then they should be strongly impressed, for the differences are both great and important. We shall make much use of these ideas in discriminating between words in the body of our book.

(4) STANDARDS and THINGS TO BE MEASURED should have special attention.   THE AUTHOR.

West Va. Univ., Morgantown, W. Va.
Sept. 1, 1907.

LATIN SYNONYMS

The lines along which we shall work will take the lead of the four special directions indicated on the last page of our preface, namely:

(1) The Generic and Specific.
(2) The Primary and Secondary.
(3) The Dynamic and Static.
(4) Standards and Things to be Measured.

FIRST CHAPTER

GENERIC AND SPECIFIC IDEAS.

Such as represent the general, common, and well-nigh universal ideas of action or condition being Generic; and those that represent special, particular and individual ideas of action or condition and of objects or subjects required in analysis for distinction being Specific. For example, there are but four absolute'y generic ideas in all the universe, but these may have sub-generics, and the sub-gener'cs may aga:n be sub-divided; but Specifics will constitute in all languages the great bu:k of all that words or symbols can represent. Hence we may conclude, that, if we learn a few hundred sub-generics, we shall have little trouble with the specifics. This we think will be made perfectly clear in the study of verbs, of which we haxe arranged many under sub-generics.

LATIN SYNONYMS

I. Generic and Specific Ideas.

(1)

Capere,	take.........the general term for 'take' in any way.
Accipere,	" ....a specific term for 'take to one's self.
Concipére,	" .... " " " 'take together' as parts of a whole or as persons performthe one act.
Decipere,	" .... " " " 'take to one side,' cheat, deceive.
Excipere,	" .... " " " 'take out' as from the original who:e, 'except,' etc., etc.
Recipere,	" .... " " " 'take back,' receive, recover, return, retain, etc., etc
Suscipere,	" .... " " " 'take up,' carry, support, endure, etc.
Percipere,	" .... " " " 'take through or thoroughly,' perceive, etc.

(2)

Habere,	have.........the general term for 'have' in any way.
Adhibere,	" ....a specific term for 'have to,' apply to, bring to, join to, add to, invite to, etc.
Cohibere,	" .... " " " 'have together,' confine, control, restrain, contain, hold, etc.
Inhibere,	" .... " " " 'have in,' hold in, restrain, check, row backward, etc.

(8)

Perhibere, have..........	."	" "	'have complete.y,' propose, say, consider, etc., etc.
Praehibere, "	"	" "	'hav、before one,' as a he'p, offer, present, furnish, afford, etc.
Prohibere, "	"	" "	'have before one,' as a h:ndrance, check, restrain, etc., etc.

(3)

| Dare, | give..........the general term for 'give' in any way whatever. |
| Abdere, | " ....a specific term for 'give away,' put away, withdraw, remove, retire, etc. |

Addere,	"	"	" "	'give to,' add to, increase, etc.
Circumdare, "	"	" "	'g ve around,' surround, etc.
Condere, "	"	" "	'give together,' put gether, form, compose, collect, etc.
Dedere, "	"	" "	'give up,' surrender, devote one's self, etc.
Edere, "	"	" "	'give out,' as from the orig'nal,. report, publish, etc., e:c.
Indere, "	"	" "	'give in,' in:roduce, put in, etc.
Perdere, "	"	" "	'give completely,' destroy, waste, etc.
Prodere, "	"	" "	'give forth,' publish, reveal, etc.

Reddere,	give..........	"	"	"	'give back,' return, reflect, resemble, repeat, etc., etc.
Subdere,	"	"	"	"	'give under,' subject, subdue, etc.
Donare,	give............the special term for making a present.				
Tradere,	" .... "	"	"	"	handing over to another what we have.
Tribuere,	" .... "	"	"	"	paying what is due.
Largiri,	" .... "	"	"	"	making gifts to friends.

(4)

Velle, wish.............a general te..n for wishing anything at all, a yielding of the mind or heart to any outgoing impulse after any desirable object that may present itself.			
Avere, wish............. or havēre (2v)	"	"	but stronger than velle, and giving us our word avarice, 'wanting the world,' never satisfied with any one thing.
Cupere, wish............a specific term for 'wishing some one thing eagerly.' From Cupere we get Cupid and Cupidity, both strong terms.			
Optare, wish............	"	"	for 'wish the best,' choose elect, etc.

Desiderare, wish..........	"	" for 'wish what one has had and lost.'
Exoptare, wish..........	"	" for 'wish eagerly the best,' an intensified optare, as though one's long-time first choice.
Concupiscere, wish.......	"	" for 'wishing eagerly and intensely one thing,' the con being the strongest intensification.

Peropto(?)

(5)

Abesse, want.............	a general term,	'away from,' as departure from some original position.
Egere, want.............	"	" denoting real need, sometimes equal to carere, sometimes equal deciderare.
Indigere "	"	" 'strong need,' absolute want, from indu = in and egere.
Carere, "	a special term,	'lacking,' having capacity for, but that capacity unfilled.
Vacare, "	"	" 'free from' something not desired.
Deesse, "	"	" 'away from,' as from something which has continued its departure or absence indefinitely
Deficere, "	"	" 'to fail,' as a resource that has lasted for a time, but no part of which is now on hand.

(6)

Ire, go................A sub-genus for action, but the most general term for 'go.'

Abire, "................to go away from any place, as one of many such departures.

Adire, "................to go to a p'ace, to approach.

Anteire, go..............to go before in t'me or to excel in action, but in general simply to precede.

Circumire, go............to go round, as in a circle, or figuratively to cheat or to express by circumlocution, or even to solicit vo'es.

Coire, "............to go together, to unite, to combine, to curdle, to freeze, or even to marry.

Deire, "............to go out, as a part from the whole.

Exire, "............to go out, as a complete organism, or as one of many important factors, the Ex belonging to those things only that indicate importance or completeness.

Inire, "............to go in, to enter, to begin, to commence, to undertake.

Interire, "............to perish, to be lost among others, to be destroyed, to die, etc., etc.

Obire, "............to come up against, to oppose, to die, and figuratively to discharge one's bail.

Perire, "............to go through, pass away, perish, die, etc., etc., the per always denoting the whole diameter of a circle or sphere.

Praeterire, "............to go by, pass by, omit, not mention, to outstrip in a race.

Prodire, go .... to go forth, go forward, advance, appear as a character in a play.

Redire, " .... to go back, come back, return, come back to one's senses, etc., etc.

Subire, " .... to come under, pass under, dive under, take upon one's self a burden, even to happen to a person, etc.

Transire, " .... to go over, but always as a whole thing from one position to another.

(7)

Venire, come .... a sub-genus for action, but the most general term for 'come.'

Advenire, come .... to come to, to happen, to come near, etc.

Antevenire, " .... to come before, to get the start, to anticipate, etc.

Circumvenire, come .... to come round, surround, beset, oppress, even to cheat.

Convenire, " .... to come together, unite, agree upon, suit, be convenient, be on good terms, etc.

Devenire, " .... to come to, arrive at, reach, as from some other position already reached.

Evenire " .... to come out, happen, befal l, occur, but always as a whole or something of great importance.

Invenire, " .... to come upon, to find or find out, to learn, but not as by searching. Reperire is used in the sense of finding by search.

Intervenire, " .... to come between, intervene, interrupt happen while something else is being done.

Obvenire, " .... to come in the way of, to meet, to happen, fall to the lot of, etc., etc.

Pervenire,	come.......	to come to, reach, attain to, etc., etc.
Praevenire,	"	to come before, anticipate, get the start of, etc.
Provenire,	"	to come forth or forward, appear upon stage, shoot forth as a plant, grow, even to succeed or prosper.
Revenire,	"	to come back, return domum or in urbem.
Subvenire,	"	to come up to aid, to help, succour, to remedy or relieve, but always close.
Supervenire,	"	to come over, to arrive, to come upon unexpectedly.
Transvenire, (?)	"	trans representing the side opposite that on which you stand, trans-ven're wou'd be an impossible idea. Trans-ire is all right, because the person can go from your side to the opposite. but he cannot "come" from your side to the side opposite you; that is 'go,' 'Come' always means toward self.

All language must be supposed to have been developed as from the standpoint of the first person.

(8)

Noscere, know............	a sub-genus of comprehension, but the general term for 'know.'
Novisse (pf.noscere) 'know'.	used as a present, perhaps because the original idea was to get possession, to grasp, and hence, 'I have grasped' (mentally), was 'to know.'
Didicisse, know...........	as 'to have learned,' being the result or effect of the causative 'teach.'
Tenere, know............	as 'to hold or possess,' being the equivalent of novisse, in that it is a present possession.

Intelligere, know ....but this is by comparison of two or more things brought before the mind. In other words, we have noted the difference.

Cognoscere, know ....a strengthened form of noscere, and so meaning thoroughly considered.

Accipere, know ....in the sense of 'receive.' I have it by its having been given to me from others; I did not get it by investigation.

Comperire, know ....as having been found out by thorough search.

Scire, know.............a shortened (?) form of noscere, the change to a fourth conjugation being made for the sake of euphony. This verb is general'y used for 'knowing by experience,' and so is opposed to opinor and arbitror.

(9)

Cogitare, think..........as to be conscious of one's ideas.

Opinari, " ....as to suppose from some view taken of an object that is brought to our attention.

Putare, " ....as counting over or estimating values, to reckon, to weigh, and hence often to believe.

Arbitrari, " ....to express an opinion as a witness, even to hear or perceive.

Censere, " ....to express an opinion as a senator, to appraise as an assessor, even to vote.

Credere, " ....to trust because of a well-grounded opinion —the half-way to knowledge.

Judicare, " ....to judge after examination has been made.

Sentire,   think.......... as to depend on the senses.
Statuere,   "   .... by coming to a fixed determination.

(10)

S'nere,   allow............ as a matter of the will, I am willing.
Pati   "   .... as a matter of weakness, I cannot help it.
Concedere,   al'ow......... as a yielding to some request.
Permittere,   "   .... as giving permission for something to be done.

(11)

Specere,   perceive........ as simply to look at, behold, or see.
Aspicere,   "   .... to look at something, to face it, even to withstand or confront, to investigate, to perceive.
Circumspicere, perceive.... to look round, to consider carefu'ly.
Conspicere,   "   ..... to look at close'y or to view as many persons at one time.
Despicere,   "   ..... to look down upon, desp'se, but often simp'y to look down from a higher position.
Inspicere,   "   ...... to look into, examine, contemplate, inspect, even to become acquainted with.
Introspicere,   "   ..... to look into closely,—(1) to be within and then (2) to look.
Perspicere,   "   ..... to look through and through, to examine thoroughly.
Prospicere,   "   ..... to look forward, to foresee, even to provide for or procure.
Respicere,   "   ..... to look back, to reflect, observe, as by going over the same ground a second or third time.

Retrospicere, .perceive..... to look backward, as by viewing at a distance things already once passed.

Suspicere, " ..... the opposite of despicere, and hence to look up to, honor, but often to merely look up from a lower position.

Transpicere, " ..... to look at something on the other side.

(12)

Sentire, perceive........ but by the senses.

Assentire, " .... (1) to perceive and then (2) to acknowledge the fact, and hence to assent.

Consentire " .... (1) to perceive and then (2) all to come to the same conclusion, and hence to agree.

Persentire, " .... to perceive distinctly or to feel deeply.

Praesentire, " .... to have a presentiment or premonition.

Subsentire, " .... to notice or perceive secretly.

Percipere, " .... to seize upon mentally, and hence to learn.

Audire, " .... through the sense of hearing alone.

Notare, " .... as by marking and then observing the marks or signs.

Animadvertere, perceive.... as by turning the whole inner man upon and about any person or thing.

Cognoscere, perceive...... as by becoming thoroughly acquainted with all the features.

Observare, " .... as by keeping the person or facts always before one's self.

Intelligere, " .... as by making comparisons of conduct today with that of yesterday or tomorrow.

(13)

Videre, perceive......... by separating one thing from all others.

Circumvidere (?) perceive.. an impossible concept, for the simple reason that videre sees only the one thing separate from others.

Evidere (?) perceive...... an impossible concept, because E means 'out from within,' and 'to see out from within' would not be separation of one thing from all others.

Invidere, " ......to look upon some one thing steadily, and hence as envious.

Pervidere, " ......to look through and through, and hence to distinguish.

Praevidere " ......to see, as it were, something immediately before us, to foresee.

Providere, " ......to see forward, and hence to provide for the one thing needed.

Revidere, " ......to see again some one thing or several considered as one.

Supervidere, " ......to supervise some one thing as distinct from a'l others, or some several things considered as one.

(14)

Cernere, perceive........by first collecting and then distributing and then selecting. See Videre above. Videre first of all, separates the one thing from all others.

Decernere, " ....is a secondary idea, and hence decision follows selection.

Discernere, " ....makes a decision or difference between any two or more of the things classified.

Excernere, " ....sorts out the one class from the other, each having its own characteristics.

Incernere, " ....sift upon, but always with the notion of collection first.

Secernere, perceive........to put asunder things that are in a collected state.

(15)

Aperire,   open.........t.to expose to view, to open up what has been concealed, but not what has been shut. Recludere is to open what has been shut.

Adaperire,   "   ....to open fully doors or gates.

Patere,   "   ....to open up by spreading out very thinly anything that has been folded up.

Hiare,   "   ....to open as by gaping, to open the mouth in astonishment, to long for.

Patefacere,   "   ....to make open or wide-spread.

Patescere,   "   ....to lie open or cause to open wide.

Reserare,   "   ....to unclose as a door, even to tear open

Perforare,   "   ....to open by piercing through, to perforate.

Recludere,   "   ....to open as gates that have been closed.

Pandere,   "   ....to open by spreading out, but not thinly.

Deicere,   "   ....to open by felling the trees.

Expandere,   "   ....to open by explaining as in giving the parts one by one.

Purgare,   "   ....to open by purifying, cleansing, etc.

Evolvere,   "   ....by unrolling what has been involved.

Inaugurare,   "   ....by getting the auspices beforehand.

Revolvere,   "   ....by rolling backward what had been roled forward.

Consecrare,   "   ....by consecrating for use a temple hitherto closed.

Resignare,   "   ....by unsealing letters or wills.

Dedicare,   "   ....by dedicating a temple hitherto unfinished.

Solvere,   "   ....by loosening what has been bound.

Discedere,	open........	caelum discedit, as the departure of clouds.
Insecare,	"	by the making of an incision.
Dehiscere,	"	by the gaping of the earth.
Incidere,	"	by bursting into a place.
Recrud'scere,	"	by wounds opening afresh.
Porrigere,	"	by stretching out the hands wide open.
Explanare,	"	by spreading out as in or on a plain.
Secare,	"	by cutting in pieces.
Detegere,	"	by taking off the roof.
Retegere,	"	by opening up the roof.
Explicare,	"	by unfolding what has been folded.
Interpretari,	"	by making distinctions between subjects hitherto confused.

(16)

Claudere, shut...........	a sub-genus of "comprehension," the general term for "close, shut in."
Circumcludere,	shut......	to shut in on all sides, circum allowing more space than con.
Concludere,	"	to shut in closely on all sides, con representing close grasp.
Excludere,	"	to shut out, but ex as heretofore meaning not to shut out a little piece of something, but to shut out some entire organism. Is there an abcludere?
Includere,	"	to shut in, but usually not a piece of anything, but some entire organism, in being employed as the opposite of ex.
Intercludere,	"	those who circumclude hold those who are intercluded, inter like circum allowing space for the things intercluded.

Occludere,	shut......	to shut up, as a house or to shut in what needs to be guarded.
Praecludere,	"	to close in front, but always with the thought of what is near at hand. The word is used for shutting a person's mouth.
Recludere,	"	to shut back, and so to open what has been closed, not what seems to have been originally encased or encrusted.
Secludere.	"	to shut off to itself, as a person or thing put in some other position or condition without or on the outside of others. Hence the word is often used in the sense of 'banish.' 'To banish cares' is curas secludere.

(17)

Ducere, lead	....	a sub-genus for 'action,' but a general term for 'lead,' 'draw,' 'drag,' the actor or doer going before.
Abducere, lead	....	to lead away from any place, condition or relation, a man from the forum, a slave from his master, a person from his allegiance, etc., etc.
Adducere,	"	just the opposite of abducere.
Circumducere, lead	....	to lead round, but not close to the things mentioned.
Conducere,	"	to lead together, and so necessarily into close connection. Con and In hold about the same relation to each other as Circum and Inter.
Deducere,	"	to lead away, as denoting that, of what has been in some original or home position, there is a departure to another position.

Educere,	lead......	to lead out, and always as we have said, some completed organism or some entire body from one place to another.
Inducere,	"	for 'putting on clothes,' but carrying, as before said, the concept of into close connection.
Introducere,	"	to introduce, the concept being that of bringing from the outside to the inside, but not necessarily into close relations.
Obducere,	"	to draw over or in front, as a cover; to wrink'e the brow, and even to spend time.
Perducere,	"	to lead or bring to any place or condition, the per carrying the meaning of all the way through, as the full diameter of circle or sphere.
Praeducere,	"	to lead forward, but differing from producere in that prae is more immediately in front than pro.
Producere,	"	to lead forward, but in the sense of going on into more distant time or space. Pro may be in the next century.
Reducere,	"	to lead back, as in returning troops to quar'ers once occupied, or to bring back to memory what once we had learned.
Seducere,	"	to lead to themselves, to exclude from the view of others.
Subducere,	"	to lead away secretly, and yet often used of hills sloping gradually downward.

Transducere, lead.........to lead over or across, as from our side of bridge or river or other separating line.

(18)

Sequi, 'follow'..........a sub-genus of "extension," the general term for 'follow.'

Adsequi, " ....to follow, but properly to follow up to that which precedes.

Consequi, " ....to follow as a consequence, either in a compact body or intently, fully, completely.

Exsequi, " ....to follow out, as something from within to the outside, and so quisque spem exsequitur, or a person follows a corpse, etc. •

Insequi, " ....to follow into and in close contact with the object pursued. Hence, to pursue an enemy.

Obsequi, " ....almost an impossible concept, but a dog often jumps up almost to the face of his master, when the dog is glad to go with the master. Here is compliance, obsequiousness.

Persequi, " ....to pursue, and, as per implies, 'all the way through.' Hence, to persecute.

Prosequi, " ....to follow forward, but in the sense of accompanying. In a hostile sense, attack or pursue.

Resequi, " ....to fo'low what has gone before, and so to answer some one by words.

Subsequi, " ....to follow close behind, and so often 'to comply with,' 'to imitate.'

(19)

Stare,	'stand'..........	the generic idea of "limitation," and the most common word in Latin for location.
Abstare,	"	to stand at a distance, reckoning from any certain point, as though having gone from that point.
Adstare,	"	to stand near, as one having come near.
Antestare,	"	to s'and before, to surpass, as simply being before, not as having gone there.
Circumstare,	'stand'......	to stand round but not near by, circum allowing much space.
Constare,	"	to stand close together, hence 'to consist of,' to stand firm, to be resolved, even to 'cost,' as we say in English.
Distare,	"	to be apart, as towers 80 feet between each other, inter and dis allowing large space.
Exstare,	"	to stand out, as something entire or representing an entirety, not as a piece of some whole thing.
Instare,	"	to stand in or on, and hence often to follow closely, to pursue.
Obstare,	"	to stand in opposition, and hence to hinder, obstruct.
Perstare,	"	to stand all the way through, to be firm, to persist, persevere.
Praestare,	"	to stand before, excel, as occupying a position, even as having an opin'on and giving that in consequence of pre-eminence.

Prostare,	'stand'......	to stand forward, as one who puts himself in that position.
Restare,	"	to stand back, in this case as never having been advanced, and hence our 'rest' as what remains or has not been used.
Substare,	"	to stand firm, as a foundation still close beneath its burden.
Superstare,	"	to stand over or upon, as occupying a pos'tion above that of sub. Super is a comparative of sub, just as in Greek Huper is the comparative of Hupo.

(20)

Sedere, 'sit'..............	a sub-genus of "limitation," the general term for 'sit' and closely related to 'stand' and 'set.'
Assidere, 'sit'............	to sit near, and hence often used for giving comfort, advice, etc.
Circumsidere, 'sit' ......} **Circumsedere,** 'sit'......}	to sit round, besiege, etc.
Considere, 'sit'............	to sit down together, in an assembly or court, but stones or timber fall to the ground, settle, sink, and waves subside.
Desidere, "	to sit away, hence to s'nk down, settle, even as mora!s, to deteriorate.
Dissidere, "	to sit apart, hence, to be distant or even hosti'e. Of clothing, not to fit.
Insidere, "	to sit upon, even to inhabit, or as birds or bees to settle, perch, or as seed to take root, etc., etc.
Obsidere, "	to sit down or remain anywhere, to blockade, besiege, invest, beset a place, etc., etc.

Persedere,	'sit'	to set le down, to remain sitting all the way through.
Praesidere,	"	to sit before and hence to act as president, to be pre-eminent, govern, manage, etc., etc.
Residere,	"	to remain sitting, to abide, stay, and even to depend upon.
Subsidere,	"	to sit down, to crouch, lie in wait, and as waves to subside.
Supersedere,	"	to sit above, remain above, and figuratively to be above doing anything, omit, leave off, etc.

(21)

Vertere,	'turn'	the general term for turn in any direction.
Advertere,	"	to turn to some one thing.
Antevertere,	"	to turn to one thing in preference to others.
Avertere,	"	to turn away from one or many things.
Circumvertere,	'turn'	to turn or twist round, even to defraud.
Convertere,	"	to turn completely round, either from one direction to the opposite or from one point in the circle or sphere to any other.
Controvertere,	"	to turn a broadside as by complete refutation.
Revertere,	"	to turn aside from the way, as in going to an inn, or to have recourse to, or to d'gress from one thought to another.
Divertere,	"	to turn away, diverge from, differ.
Evertere,	"	to overturn, throw down, raze to the foundations, even to turn up the waters by the winds.

Invertere,	turn	to turn over, turn upside down, transpose, alter, pervert, etc., etc.
Intervertere,	"	to embezzle, to turn what belonged to one over to another, to defraud, even to spend or lavish one's own.
Introvertere (?)	"	to turn wrong side out.
Obvertere,	"	to turn towards or against, to oppose.
Pervertere,	"	to turn thoroughly, turn upside down.
Praevertere,	"	to undertake before or in preference, to cause to turn, preoccupy.
Revertere,	"	to turn back, revert to previous statements or a former discourse, as well as come back to persons or places.
Subvertere,	"	to overthrow, ruin, destroy, by putting what was at the bottom on top.
Transvertere,	"	to turn across, as by making a vertical to become horizontal, and vice versa.

(22)

Cedere, 'go'		'proceed,' or 'retire,' as the general term for yielding to an overpowering influence.
Accedere, 'go'		to approach, even to be added as increase.
Antecedere, 'go'		to go before in space or time, sometimes to overtake.
Concedere,	"	to go away, depart, withdraw, to yield to, the Con being intensive or representing more than one actor.
Decedere,	"	to go away, as by yielding to necessity or fate.

Discedere,   go.......... to go asunder, separate into two parts, even to come out of a contest victor or vanquished.

Excedere,   " .... to go out, as a whole from that which has confined one's operations, hence often used of digression from a subject.

Incedere,   " .... to go in, but as entering upon what may be a doubtful contest or a difficult enterprise.

Intercedere,   " .... to go between, but always with the idea that it is the less or the weaker before the greater or the stronger.

Occedere,   " .... to meet, as by going into the presence or even the sight of a person.

Praecedere,   " .... to go before, as a ranking officer, and hence often carrying the concept of surpassing some other person.

Procedere,   " .... to go forward, and often as turning out well or prosperously.

Recedere,   " .... to recede, as giving way to powers with which we can no longer contend.

Secedere,   " .... to withdraw, as a part to itself.

Succedere,   " .... to follow, as coming up close behind, and always with the thought of inferiority, at least for the time being, to the forces with which we meet or may meet on the way.

Supercedere (?) 'go'...... to go to the higher position, but with the idea of having occupied the lower.

(23)

Gradi, 'step'.............. as the general term for 'walk' or 'go' by the upward and forward movement.

Aggredi,	'step'..........	to go to or approach, either to address a person or to make an attack, often simp y to begin an undertaking.
Antegredi,	"	to go on before, either in time or place.
Circumgredi,	'step'........	to go round, especially with hostile intent.
Congredi,	"	to meet, not as in concedere, but as equals, either as enemies or simply as disputants.
Degredi,	"	to step down, to descend from mountain to p ain, even to dismount from a horse.
Digredi,	"	to depart, as from the beaten track or even as the moon not keeping up with the sun.
Egredi,	"	to go out, as from any large space, but always with the idea of a whole and not as a piece of any whole.
Ingredi	"	to go in or into, to enter upon a journey, to commence a speech.
Introgredi,	"	to enter, not as onto a line, but as within the boundaries of some enclosure.
Praegredi,	"	to go before, as a superior, and so to outstrip. Sometimes used for going beyond or marching past in the sense of praetergredi.
Praetergredi,	"	to go beyond, as in marching.
Progredi,	"	to go forward, to advance as an equal from one position to another.
Regredi,	"	to go back, as an army in retreat, but rather as retracing its steps, not as having been conquered.

Retrogredi,   'step'..........to move backwards instead of forwards, but not as those who are compelled thus to move.

Subgredi,   "   ....to go to for attack, and hence to get c.ose, even though on lower ground.

Supergredi,   "   ....to pass above, that is ,to take a position higher or better than that occupied by another.

Transgredi,   "   ....to pass over, that is, to the other side or the other party.

(24)

Mittere, 'send'............the general term for transmitting from ourselves through others information or property.

Admittere, 'send'.........to let go, to turn over, as it were, the reins to a horse, to give a person the privilege of an audience or even to share an undertaking.

Circummittere, 'send'......to send in a roundabout way or in all directions.

Committere,   "   ......to unite, as forces in a battle, to entrust, as the neck to the barber.

Demittere,   "   ......to let down, to lead on an army to a lower position, to sail down a river, even to let one's self down, to become discouraged.

Dimittere,   "   ......to send in different directions, to let things go through the fingers, to leave or abandon a siege, etc., etc.

Emittere,   "   ......to send out, as soldiers from a fort or station, as sounds from the throat, as a debtor from his debt, etc., etc.

Immittere,	'send'......	to send in, as vessels into fight, as cavalry for attack, as darts against an enemy, etc., etc.
Intermittere,	"	to leave space between, to abandon for a time, to let time pass, etc., etc.
Intromittere,	"	to send in, as legiones in hostem.
Omittere,	"	to let go, as though o in omittere were an equal av equal ab, and meant 'away.'
Permittere,	"	to let go, as horses against an enemy, to surrender as power to any one, to make allowance for, as for anger, etc.
Praemittere,	"	to send before, as dispatches or troops.
Praetermittere,	"	to let pass, as neglecting time or opportunity.
Promittere,	"	to let go forward, and hence to promise.
Remittere,	"	to let go back, and hence to loosen the reins, to give up, to abate.
Submittere,	"	to let myself down, to send the eyes up from below (we say to look up), even to produce.
Transmittere,	"	to let pass over, to lead from one point to another, to leave unnoticed, to entrust to another, etc., etc.

(25)

Emere, 'take'............	but generally used for 'buy' or 'purchase.'
Sumere, 'take up'........	as to take to one's self any piece of property that may be bought, borrowed or hired, and even to assume what may not be natural.

Assumere, 'take up'......to take for one's assistance, as from another source, to claim, as something belonging to one's self.

Consumere,   "   ....to take up completely, and hence to use up, to waste, to destroy.

Desumere,   "   .... to choose or select, as anything from a secondary source, even as enemies for one's self.

Insumere,   "   ....to take for anything, as time or money for the accomplishment of a purpose.

Praesumere,   "   .... to take beforehand, as remedies or as food, to anticipate, to imagine, take for granted, etc., etc.

Resumere,   "   ....to take again, as tablets for writing; to renew, as a battle; to recover, as strength, etc., etc.

(26)

Ponere, 'put, place'......the general term for 'put' or 'place' any where, but specifically down as on a level.

Anteponere,   'put, place'..to put before, as dinner for some one; to put before, as in front of others; to prefer, as friendship to all human things.

Apponere,   "   ..to put to, as to add years to life; to serve, as a dish for the table; to count as gain, as to put on the debit side, etc. etc.

Circumponere,   "   ..to put round, as to encircle a grove or to put troops around a city.

Componere,   "   ..to put together, compose, settle, compare, dispose of things that are scattered.

Deponere,	'put, place' ..	to put down, as the head on the earth; to lay, as a wager or as a prize; to lay aside, as an office; to lay up, as money.
Exponere,	" ..	to set forth, as in explanation; to land troops, as from a ship; to expose for sale, as wares or produce in the market.
Imponere,	" ..	to put in, as some one in a sepulcher; to put on ship, as soldiers for another country; to impose upon, as to cheat, wrong, and defraud.
Interponere,	" ..	to put between, as anything that may or should occupy intervening space or time.
Opponere,	" ..	to put opposite, as men for their country; to oppose, as an argument, etc.
Postponere,	" ..	the opposite of anteponere, and so to put behind what should be before.
Praeponere,	" ..	to put before, as a commander for the troops, the thought being that he is in close touch with the troops.
Proponere,	" ..	to put forward, as that which may be seen, but not implying nearness to the eyes, to report, as news, etc., etc.
Reponere,	" ..	to put back, as to restore anything to i s place; to recline, as at the table on the left elbow; to cause to rest, as hope in virtue, etc., etc.
Seponere,	" ..	to put to itself, and hence to separate from others for a purpose, as the captured money for building a temple.

Supponere,	'put, place'	..to put under, as eggs under hens; to sow, as the teeth of vipers; to forge, as false wills.
Superponere,	"	..to put over, as an ornament to the head; to set up, as in a station of authority.
Transponere,	"	..to transport, as soldiers about to go into a foreign land.

(27)

Esse,	'be'	............as the general term for continued consciousness. The perfect fui is closely connected with our verb 'be' and carries the concept of 'origin.'
Abesse,	"	to be away, as from any one of many positions.
Adesse,	"	to be present, as at some certain place.
Deesse,	"	to be wanting, as failing to be present for duty.
Inesse,	"	to be in or on, as a fault in our characters, or as a blot on our escutcheon.
Interesse	"	to be between, as of time or space; to be present and take part in, as at a feast; to be interested, as in noting differences.
Obesse,	"	to be in the way, as prejudicial to; to hinder, as occupying the road to be passed over.
Praeesse,	"	to be at the head of, as a commander of troops. Caesar uses the word often in connection with his commanders.
Prodesse,	'be'	to be useful, as the opposite of obesse.

Subesse, 'be'............to be behind or near at hand, as the
day is near, just after the first light
comes from the east; to be in question, to exist, as when no suspicion of
danger is thought of.

Superesse, " ....to be over and above, as a remnant or
as a superfluity, and hence after a
battle, Caesar said so many super-
fuerunt.

(28)

Agere, 'do'..............the most general term for 'action' to
be found in the Latin, the same root
ag being found also in Greek.

Abigere, 'do'............to drive away, as birds or beasts; to
banish or get rid of, as to remove
whatever is troublesome or in one's
way.

Adigere, " ....to drive to, as cattle from other places
to our place; to summon a.man to
court, to swear him in, etc., etc.

Ambigere, " ....to go about or around, and hence to-
dispute or contend at law or other-
wise, even to doubt, hesitate, or be
uncertain.

Circumagere, 'do'........to drive or turn round in a circle, as
persons or animals. The master who
freed his slave took the slave by the
right hand and turned him round.

Degere, " ....to pass time, as in spending some definite remaining time of life.

Exigere. " ....to drive out, as persons or animals
from some place, to complete or
finish, as a monument; to demand, as
money.

Peragere,	'do'........	to pierce through, and hence to complete.
Praeteragere,	"	to drive past, as a horse beyond any designated spot.
Redigere,	"	to drive back, as the cavalry of the enemy; to bring back, as something to one's memory.
Retroagere,	"	to drive back, as men or animals from their wanderings.
Subigere,	"	to drive under, as swine under the shade; to compel one to act against his will, as men to surrender.
Transigere,	"	to drive through, as by stabbing with a sword; to finish, as a business in hand; to put an end to a dispute, etc.

(29)

Facere,	'make'..........	sub-generic to agere, to do some definite work, as to make a table or book, etc.
Afficere,	"	sub-specific to abigere, and so to affect or influence either body or mind.
Benefacere,	'make'........	to do well, as one who undertakes to do nothing otherwise.
Conficere,	"	to complete some definite action, and hence to destroy.
Deficere,	"	to rebel or revolt, as from a king; to fail, as acting away from our proper sphere; to be discouraged, and hence. to abandon.
Efficere,	"	to effect or produce, as some complete outgoing of our efforts.
Inficere,	"	to infect, as to operate upon the hidden springs of life, and hence to poison.

Interficere, "make".........to kill, as by making openings in the body, as it were space between vital organs or parts of the body.

Malefacere, " ....the oppos'te of benefacere, and hence to do ill in any possible way.

Officere, " ....to be in the way of, as grasses or weeds in the way of growing vegetab es, as a man in the way of his neighbor.

Perficere, " ....to finish, as by making what was out-lined a complete work.

Praeficere, " ....to put in charge, as a commander who shall be in close touch with those whom he leads.

Proficere, " ....to make forward, as by making proofs of efficiency or of being advantageous.

Proficisci, " ....to go forward, as in setting out on a journey, and even of proceeding from a place as a source.

Reficere, " ....to remake, restore, refit, reform, re-build, etc., as doing over what has been undone.

Sufficere, " ....to provide or supply, as by bringing up what has been lost and so replacing as it were from the lower ranks or levels what has gone from the higher.

(30)

Ferre, 'carry'...........the most general term for 'transfer,' and found in more forms in a l the Aryan tongues than any other word.

Adferre, 'carry'.........to bring to a person or place, as an addi'ion to what one has as news, as a favor or as an injury.

Anteferre, 'carry'......... to put in front what has never been behind.

Auferre, " .... to carry away, and hence to steal, even to draw a person away from his purpose.

Circumferre, 'carry'...... to carry round, as the eyes in all directions, to spread reports, etc., etc.

Conferre, " ...... to bring together, either for good or bad purposes, to contribute money, to unite strength, or to fight hand to hand.

Deferre, " ...... to bear away or down, as anything from one place to another.

Efferre, " ...... to bring out, to publish, remove, any complete thing from its surroundings.

Gerere, " ...... to carry on, not as ferre, 'to transfer,' but to carry continually as a knife in the pocket.

Inferre, " ...... to bring in or upon, as force against an enemy or as favor to friends.

Introferre, " ...... to bring within, as food from without for the household.

Obferre, " ...... to offer, as to bring one's self or other help to friends or against enemies, by putting one's self immediately in front.

Perferre, " ...... to carry through as by completing the whole diameter of a circle or sphere, even to suffer to the end.

Postferre, " ...... the opposite of anteferre, hence, instead of preference, there is little value placed on the thing mentioned.

Praeferre, " ...... to carry in front, as a torch and always close to one's self.

Proferre,	'carry'	to carry forth or forward, and hence to bring to light or reveal.
Praeterferre,	"	to carry past the goal or some designated point.
Referre,	"	to carry back, and so to report, even to restore to a former condition.
Subferre,	"	to carry, as a person being underneath, and hence to endure as suffering.
Superferre.	"	to carry over or beyond, as by going over a mountain with the burden on the shoulders.
Transferre,	"	to carry over, but not above, only to the other side.

SECOND CHAPTER

PRIMARY AND SECONDARY IDEAS.

Such as represent first thoughts on any subject, as **One** in counting, as **I** in pronouns, as **of** and **up** in Prepositions, as **am** and **is** in verbs, etc., etc. being **Primary**; and those that represent necessarily secondary thoughts, as **Two** in counting, as **Thou** in pronouns, as **Down** and **Through** in prepositions, as **See** and **Seek** in verbs, etc., etc., being **Secondary**.

We have merely introduced the subject in a few pages, so as to open the way for further investigations, and will often refer to these pages in the body of the work, so that the student may become well grounded in the principles and may carry the analysis into other languages, if he so elects.

II. PRIMARY AND SECONDARY IDEAS.

Agere, 'set in motion' is **primary** as shown by its definition, and represents the most general term for action of any kind.

Degere, 'pass onward,' is **secondary** as shown by its definition and represents the specific action of passing over that part of a road yet untraveled.

The following **Prepositions** exhibit very clearly the characteristics of **Primaries:**

Ad, 'to,' with gerundives indicates the purpose of the undertaking and this in general is extended into 'to place' to be reached as a matter of anticipation or as a fact remembered The Ad idea is always primary with reference to the De idea. Hence **De** is secondary.

Ab, 'from,' as from border or boundary, and indicating the outcome of only part of any inner power or strength. For example, a sole means the heat and light coming little by little; a Caesare is the use of only part of Caesar's energy.

Ante, 'before, primary and representing the position occupied or to be occupied before any other position that may be conceived.

Adversus, 'toward,' 'against,' as meeting any person or thing on our line of movement. **Contra** represents opposition in every direction,—a "broadside."

Adversum, 'toward,' 'against,' as the neuter form of adversus, represents the general and not the specific opposition.

Apud, 'at,' 'near,' indicates the fitness of the presence. The person who is apud me or apud populum is for the time being where he should be. He is a guest of honor and feels welcome.

Ob, 'against, on account of,' indicates the facing of an object which is near at hand. Used with general and not special objects, as for examples, **ob rem,** but not **ob spem.** We say **propter spem,** and **quam ob rem,** because **ob,** except sometimes in poetry, goes with general and not with specific ideas. **Propter spem** is 'on account of' hope yet to be realized, while **Ob** goes back to an affair or cause already known and estimated.

E or **ex,** 'from,' but 'out from within,' particularly as partaking largely of what is within, as exhibiting all the essential qua ities or characteristics of the w'thin.

In, 'in, into,' always represents a position taken or to be taken as only part of the space referred to. **In** holds about the same relation to **con** that **inter** holds to **circum.** **In** and **Con** allow less space than **inter** and **circum.**

Inter, 'between,' being a position as closely re ated to the one object as to the other, and hence often expressing the idea of reciprocity. **Inter annos** means during the years ,but in the sense of as much connec'ed with one as with the other. **Inter** and **circum** allow large space.

Erga, 'towards,' as in a first movement of one's feelings, good or bad, out toward a person or thing, general'y used with reference to favorable outgoings, occasional y for feelings of hate; but as a general term, it is capab'e of use in either a good or bad sense.

The following **Prepositions** exhibit just as clearly the characteristics of **Secondaries:**

De, 'of, from,' but always after some position has been reached, and hence secondary showing usually a change of direction from the original line. For example, water taken out from wi'h'n a reservoir is **Ex** from the reservoir, while just flowing from the side of the reservoir it is **Ab** from the reservoir; but, after running some distance in the main pipe when it turns off in'o another pipe up or down, to right or left, it goes on by **De.**

Secundum, 'after,' as following, coming next, but behind. Derived from **Sequens,** and hence secondary and never primary. Its neuter form makes it generic and not specific.

Subter, 'under,' but not 'near' as would be represented by **sub.** Sub touches that which it is under, but subter may be an inch or a mile below that which is mentioned. The -ter is a comparative termination and hence shows a greater distance below than is indicated by sub, the positive form Sub and then super, going upward; sub and then subter, going downward.

Trans, 'over,' 'across, representing a secondary with reference to this side which is primary. The thought is that the thing or the person as a whole has changed places so that what was here is now there the thr of English being equal to tr of the Latin and used as a secondary demonstrative element. Trans is always opposite to the position you occupy, and so transvenire is an impossible concept. See page 14.

The following **Conjunctions** also show **Primary** ideas as differing from **Secondaries:**

Et, 'and,' a loose, slipshod connective, which can be used between any two objects,—between elephant and spade, between mountain and buggy, because as a conjunction it gives only the thought of simple addition. The enclitics —que connects objects considered of the same value. Hence neither of the objects is secondary.

Aut, 'or,' another loose connective which may be used between any two objects, and therefore a primary 'or.'

At, 'but,' always primary and therefore bringing in a new thought or a new speaker. Sed is always secondary and therefore is an addition to or extension of the same person's thought.

Ita, 'in this manner,' as a primary method and representing the first thought with reference to some action or condit'on which is extended into or up to what the grammars call 'result' or 'purpose.'

Ut, 'that,' is also primary and a modification of the form and use and purpose of **Ad,**—primary because the result was foreshadowed or foreseen in the **ita,**—primary because the purpose was formed before the action was undertaken.

Sic, 'so,' is d'stinctly secondary, as is shown in examples representing a secondary thought compared with the primary introduced by **Ut.**

The following **Conjunctions** exhibit just as clearly the characteristics of **secondaries:**

Sive or Seu, 'or,' used to connect a primary and a secondary concept, the secondary of course following.

Vel or Ve, 'or,' connect objects regarded as of the same value, and you can have your choice. Hence neither is secondary, unless you depend on the position of the words.

Sed, 'but,' always secondary, as giving some addition to a thought already partly expressed,—never used to bring in an entire'y new thought.

Neque or Nec, 'not,' like all negatives, is necessarily secondary, for a negat've, no ma'ter whether conjunction or adverb, is impossible as an idea before there has been an affirmation. See "Philosophy of Expression."

We have not introduced the hundredth part of what could be brought under **Primary** and **Secondary** ideas, but enough we hope to start the student in his thinking on the differences that can be readily discovered between words that are necessarily primary and others just as necessarily secondary. We w'll frequently mention the subject of this·section in he pages that follow, so that the thought we would impress may become perfectly clear to every student.

THIRD CHAPTER

DYNAMIC AND STATIC IDEAS.

Those being dynamic wh'ch express thoughts of outcome, avail-
ability, potency as resulting from organ'sm or combination giving
the capacity for gathering and maintaining a static supply; and those
being static, which, as having capacity from organism or combination, possess the power latent, inclusive, and ready for use when
some call is made. For examples, what we call strength is static
and inherent, and may or may not be used for purposes best for
ourselves, and yet at least a part of the static strength will work
out somewhere, somehow, even though by disease; while what we
call force or power is dynamic and available, and so shows itself
in work or speech or song or play.

III. DYNAMIC AND STATIC IDEAS.

Vis, 'force'.............. is distinctly **dynamic,** for it always represents that which must phenomenize or manifest itself in word or deed or product.

    (See also **Vi-ta, vi-vo,** so named from manifested power.)

Robur, 'strength'.......... is distinctly **static,** for it always represen s that which is latent and back of **vis.**

Posse, 'able'............. **dynamic,** for such power must be
Pollere, 'able.'   proven by some manifestation.

    This is the ability to do anything, and hence most generally carrying two ideas, (1) That of **Posse;** (2) That of **valere;** and hence not on y manifesting itself, but also accomplishing a purpose. It is **pragmatic.**

Valere, 'able'............. **dynamic,** but generally used for accomplishing some particular work.

Quire, 'able'............. **Static,** for such strength is the inner,
    the Eng. 'Can,'   the conscious, but not necessarily
    the Ger., 'Konnen,'   manifested in any word or deed or
    the A S., 'Cann,'   product. It is latent and only known
    the Sansc., 'Gna.'   to the individual that possesses it.
    the Greek, 'Gno.'   When it is manifested, then it be-
    etc., etc., etc.   comes known by the expression posse or pollere or valere.

Posse and **Valere** and **Pollere** and **V's** are known and recognized by the Objective mind, while **Robur (Hrobur)** and **Quire** are known only by the Subjective mind. The Saxon mind was always more subjective than that of the Roman. The Roman, living in a land where the summers were long and vegetation and outdoor life were always claiming his attention, became more and more given up to the outer world of nature and to the social and artistic sides of existence, and hence, like the Greek, if he had gods, they too must come before his objective mind in numerous images. He must have something to see or he cou d not worship, and today images and pictures adorn the Cathedral walls everywhere in Italy. But the Saxon, shut in by fog and rain and snow, became more subjective in his thinking and hence ab'e to conceive of God and Good as absolute entities, whether he could see either or not.

We have simply introduced here the subject of **Dynamic** and **Static** ideas, but in the pages that follow we will often refer to this section, so that the student will get a clear insight to the d fference that exists between these important classifications of thought and speech.

Adjective Terminals.

The value of these terminals is highly important in distinguishing synonyms.

—aceus, material or origin.

—alis, per aining to whatever the root or stem expresses.

—aris, pertaining to whatever the root or stem expresses.

—anus, belonging to whatever the root or stem expresses.

—as, belonging to whatever the root or stem expresses.

—arius, one of or belonging to whatever the root or stem expresses.

—atilis, one of or belonging to whatever the root or stem expresses.

—atus, ma er al of which made.

—ax, propensity by nature.

—ber, bringing or bearing whatever the root or stem expresses.

—bilis, possibility of anything in the passive.

—bundus, full of whatever the root or stem expresses.

—culus, the diminutive of whatever the root or stem expresses.

—eusis, belonging to whatever the root or stem expresses.

—ianus, belonging to whatever the root or stem expresses

—cosus, fulness of whatever the root or stem expresses.

—cundus, fulness of whatever the root or stem expresses.

—ellus, diminutive of whatever the root or stem expresses.

—er, extension of whatever the root or stem expresses.

—eus, material or similar to whatever the root or stem expresses.

—icius, material or origin.

—icus, quality of whatever the root or stem expresses.

—idus, quality of whatever the root or stem expresses.

—ilis, possibility of anything in the passive sense.

—ilis, possibility of anything in the passive sense.

—ineus, pertaining to whatever the root or stem expresses.

—inus, belonging to whatever the root or stem expresses

—ius, belonging to whatever the root or stem expresses.

—lentus, full of whatever the root or stem expresses.

—olus, diminutive of whatever the root or stem expresses.

—ples, fulness of whatever the root or stem expresses.

—s, extension of whatever the root or stem expresses.

—ster, place of abode.

—ulus, propensity to whatever the root or stem expresses.

—uus, fulness of whatever the root or stem expresses.

—uosus, fulness of whatever the root or stem expresses.

—us, completeness or fulness of whatever the root or stem expresses.

(37)

Adjectives.

(366)

Malus,   'bad'............as a direct opposite to **bonus. Malus** is the general term for anything bad.

Adversus,   "   ....as turned against us and opposing us, but on a line rather than on all sides.

Foedus, 'bad'............as foul.
Difficilis,   "   ....as hard or difficult to get on with.
Incommodus, 'bad'.........as inconvenient, iter incommodus.
Adulterius,   "   ....as spurious, and so applicable to money.
Aeger,   "   ....as sick, homo aeger.
Pravus,   "   ....as naturally depraved, and hence morally irresponsible
Turpis,   "   ....as base, and hence belonging to turba.
Depravatus,   "   ....as having been rendered depraved by environment.
Nequam,   "   ....indeclinable, and equal to ne + aequus, as a negative, born bad and never good.
Iniquus,   "   ....as a privative, born good, but temporarily bad.
Asper,   "   ....as rough to the touch.
Maledicus,   "   ....as uttering bad language.
Malitiosus,   "   ....as full of malice.
Malevolus,   "   ....as wishing evil.
Malignus,   "   ....as born bad, of bad disposition.
Maleficus,   "   ....as an evil doer.

Acceptus,   'pleasant'......what is pleasant to see or hear.
Amoenus,   "   ......because delightful to the eyes.
Carus,   "   ......because dear to us.
Dulcis,   "   ......because attractive.
Facetus,   "   ......because witty.
Festivus,   "   ......because humorous.
Gratus,   "   ......because always active for us.
Fecundus,   "   ......because full of good cheer.
Lepidus,   "   ......because charming to us.
Laetus,   "   ......because joyous.
Suavis,   "   ......because odorous to the sense of smell or sweet to that of taste.

Beatus,   'happy'..........opp. to miser, as of one who has been
                            blessed.

Bonus,   "   ....opp. to malus, as of one good in every
                            particular. Bonus is the general
                            term for anything good.

Faustus,   "   ....as of business which has been favored
                            by the omens.

Felix,   "   ....as of one whose wishes are always ful-
                            fil'ed.

Fortunatus, "   ....one who has been favored outwardly by
                            Fortuna.

Prosperus, "   ....as of things according to one's hopes.

Secundus,   "   ....opp. to adversus, following one's
                            wishes or plans.

Aptus,   "   ....because seeming to fit completely into
                            plans.

Accommodatus, happy'.....because made for advantage.

Gratus, 'happy'..........because it is pleasing to the opposite
                            parties.

Novus   'new'............what is now known, but was not known
                            before.

Recens,   "   ....what is fresh or recently made or pro-
                            duced.

Inauditus   "   ....what has not been heard of before.

Insolitus, "   ....as of something to which we have not
                            been accustomed before.

Parvus, 'small'..........the most general term for small in all
                            dimensions.

Tenuis,   "   ....as something thin.

Exiguus,   "   ....as of something reduced in lateral di-
                            mensions.

Minutus, 'small'.........as of something having been diminished.

Pusillus, " ....as of the condition of the soul, little in power.

Angustus, " ....as something narrow, like a road.

Gracilis, " ....as something slim or slender.

Parum Magnus, 'small'....a litotes for 'quite small.'

Nobilis, 'noble'..........as by birth.

Liberalis, " ....as belonging to a freeman.

Generosus, " ....as of one naturally great and good.

Clarus, " ....as by reputation for distinguished ability.

Honestus, " ....because of having been honored.

Ingenuus, " ....because of inborn virtues.

Insignis, " ....because distinguished by active goodness.

Corpore amplo, 'thick'.....a body particularly large in width.

Concretus, thick........as of that which has seemingly grown together. Often used of curdled milk.

Confertus, " ....as of things brought together in a mass, being opposed to rarus.

Creber, " ....as of persons who have assembled in a body.

Callosus, " ....as a callous or hardened skin.

Crassus, " ....opposed to tenuis, and hence stout or compact.

Densus, ' " ....as of many persons standing near each other.

Durus. " ....as that by which hardness or lastingness acquires the kindred concept of thickness.

Fréquens, 'thick'............as of persons who have come together from different directions.

(Vox) Obtusa, " ....as a voice that has been blunted by being struck, as it were, on the point.

Obesus, " ....as a fat person, one well-fed.

Pinguis, " ....as a plump person or animal.

Spissus, " ....as being impenetrable, opposed to soîutus. Used of soil, of darkness, etc.

Turgens, " ....as seemingly swelling.

Turgidus, " ....as being already swollen.

Silens, 'silent'............as being free from noise.

Tacitus, " ....as being without speech.

Taciturnus, 'silent'........as being disposed to say nothing.

Agrestis, 'of the country...as being like the fields in their natural state Hence rough.

Rusticus, " " ...as having the manners of the country, hence uncouth.

Rusticanus, " " ...as leading temporarily the life of the country.

Incolumis, 'safe'..........as having received no damage.

Integer, " ....as having been untouched by harm.

Salvus, ' " ....as having been delivered from harm, which without a deliverer would have destroyed.

Securus, " ....as being free from care.

Sospes, " ....as never having been harmed, even though passing through many dangers unscathed.

Tutus, " ....as protected from danger.

illaesus

Coelebs, single'............... as an unmarried man.

Singularis, 'single'......... opp. to plures, and hence standing alone

Unus, 'one'............... as an individual among many.

Unicus, 'only'.. ?........... as an only son, no other sons in the 'family.

Solus, 'alone'.............. as an individual apart from any others

Singulus, 'one alone'....... as one at a time.

Dispar, 'unlike'........... as being unequal in length, bread'h, or th ckness, or in strength, or in other qualities.

Dissimilis, " .... as being unlike in shape or features.

Certior, 'more cer'a'n'..... as being better known from effects.

Nobilior, 'better reputation'. as being better known by birth

Notior, 'better marked'..... as being better known by distinction.

Hostilis, 'like an enemy'... as being of hostile mind.

Infestus, " " ... as not ward'ng off attacks.

Inimicus, " " ... as being the true opposite of amicus, and so as a friend will help, an enemy wi l hinder; as a friend loves. so an enemy hates.

Insciens, 'ignorant'...... temporarily, and not blameworthy.

Nesciens. " ...... and never having been otherwise.

Inscius, " ...... absolutely ignorant of some one thing, but not implying inability to be otherwise.

Inscitus, " ...... as having been thus conceived or shaped.

Imprudens, " ...... as not seeing anything pertaining to the future.

Insipiens, " ...... unwise temporarily.

Ignarus, " ...... absolute unconsciousness of some fact.

Ignorans,	'ignorant'......	temporary unconsciousness of some fact.
Imperitus,	"	......absolute unskilfulness from want of experience.
Indoctus,	"	......as one never having been taught, but not implying inability to learn.
Illiteratus,	"	......as one never having studied books.
Nescius,	"	......absolutely ignorant of some one thing, and implying inability to be otherwise.
Rudis,	"	......as implying an uncultivated state.
Stultus,	' "	......as a fool who never did nor can know anything.
Carus,	'dear'.........	as an object of great interest or affection.
Pretiosus,	"	.........as an object of great value.
Aptissimus,	'best'.........	as best suited to ourselves or others.
Optimus,	"	.........as most choice.
Anxius,	'anxious'.........	as being brought into straits and being unable to free oneself from fear or difficulty.
Permotus,	"	.........as being greatly moved by excitement.
Perturbatus,	"	.........as greatly disturbed by mental fear.
Sollicitus,	"	.........as wholly agitated, completely under the power of mental or physical fear.
Afflictus,	'sad'.........	as having been damaged by some misfortune.
Debilitatus,	"	.........as having been weakened by disease.
Maerens,	"	.........as one mourning over some loss.

Maestus,	'sad'..........	as having been caused to mourn or causing mourning, but by bringing dejection and not by outcries.
Miser,	"	opp. of beatus, and hence feeling oneself unfortunate.
Tristis,	"	opp. of 'aetus, and hence gloomy and not glad.
Infelix,	"	because the wishes are unfu'filled.
Infortunatus,	"	not favored outwardly by Fortuna.
Lugens,	"	as shown by cries and outward signs.
Lugubris,	"	as bringing, or bearing, or causing expressions of grief.

Cemens,	'mild'..........	as a merciful judge, or as quiet water.
Dulcis,	"	as pleasant to any one of the senses.
Faci'is,	"	as gentle in manners or easy to deal with.
Indulgens	"	as being favorable to persons or other objects.
Lenis,	"	as gentle in effect.
Levis,	"	as opposed to gravis.
Mansuetus,	"	as tame, and hence subject to rules.
Misericors,	"	as svmpathe'ic by nature.
Mitis,	"	as carrying in itself the quality of gentleness.
Mollis,	"	as in itself pliable and incapable of rough effect.
Placidus,	"	as be'ng pleasing, flowing gently.
Tener,	"	as being young or fresh.

Praegnans,	'pregnant'.....	as present'ng signs of coming birth.
Gravis,	"	as simply heavy with young.
Gravidus,	"	as having become fil'ed with anything.
Gravidatus,	"	as having been fi led by planting seed.

Pressus, . 'pregnant'......as pressed down and hence loaded with.

Fetus, . . ' " ......as fi.led with. See Virgil's Machina
　　　　　　　feta armis.

Aberrans, 'wandering'.....wandering away from an original
　　　　　　　home.

Devius, " .....as having missed 'he road.

Dissipatus, " .....is hav'ng been scattered before hand.

Dispersus, " .....is having been scattered, but trying to
　　　　　　　come together.

Delirus, " .....is an ox that has gone out of the fur-
　　　　　　　row.

Errans, " .....as now moving without destinat'on.

Deerrans, " .....as continu'ng to wander aimlessly.

Errabundus, " ....having the dispos'tion and habit of
　　　　　　　wandering.

Peregrinans, " .....traveling in foreign countries. .

Palans, . " .....roving, straying, as cattle over the
　　　　　　　fields. .

Vagans, " .....going from place to place.

Vagrans, " .....going from field to field.

Vagus, . . " .....as aim'ess in one's work.

Celeber, 'numerous'......as being full of people.

Creber, " ......from cresco, and hence crowded to-
　　　　　　　gether.

Frequens, " .....as having come to one place from many
　　　　　　　directions.

Numerosus, " ......as indiv'duals counted one by one.

Multiplex, " ......as consisting of many folds, but not as
　　　　　　　units

Abjectus, 'low'..........as having been cast down from a higher
　　　　　　　position.

Humilis,	'low'..........	as to the position occupied or condi tion of birth.
Demissus,	"	as being dispir:ted.
Ignob.lis,	"	as to birth and ancestors.
Illiberalis,	"	as unwoithy a freeborn citizen.
Inferior,	"	as to position.
Gravis,	"	as to the voice, as base.
Obscurus,	"	as to birth and ances ors.
Submissus,	"	as to the voice, as weak.
Sordidus,	"	as to origin.
Suppressus,	"	as to the voice, as a whisper.
Vilis,	"	as to the price.
Tenuis,	"	as to property.
Turpis,	"	as belonging to the crowd, base.
Caducus,	'fleeting'........	because always incl'ned to fall.
F uxus,	"	because always inclined :o flow away.
Fugax,	"	because by nature inclined to flee away.
Volatilis,	"	because inclined to fly away.
Vo:aticus,	"	because having the power to fly away.
Pugnax,	'pugnacious'......	as being by nature inclined to fight.
Ferax,	".	as being by nature like a wi'd beast.
Bell:còsus,	"	as being full of the war spirit.
Belliger,	"	as having a mart:al disposition.
Tenax,	'tenacious'........	because inc'ined by nature to hold on.
Cons'ans,	"	because always being the same.
Fide'is,	"	because inclined to keep his word.
Astutus,	'shrewd'........	as cunning or tricky in methods.
Callidus,	"	as knowing by experience.
Perspicax,	"	as natural'y or by instinct seeing through one's surroundings.
Prudens,	"	as foreseeing results or effects.

So lers,   'shrewd'........as be'ng complete in all arts.
Sagax,   "   ....as naturally inclined to acuteness of
                                mental vision.

Egregius,   'fine'..........as the pick of the flock.
Elegans,   "   ....as selec:ed from any number of things.
Exquisitus,   "   ....as carefully sought from original
                                sources.
Conquisitus, "   ....as carefully sought from all p'aces.
Venustus,   "   ....as possessing all the qualities of Venus.
Bellus,   "   ....as a diminutive of bonus, equal to
                                pretty.
Acutus,   "   ....as having a sharp point; mentally, of
                                fine perception
Argutus,   "   ....as sign'ficant of power or mental in-
                                fluence.
Liberalis,   "   ....as belonging to the arts.
Subtilis,   "   ....as some'hing finely woven; mentally
                                of fine ability.
Serenus,   "   ....as the weather, the sky, the night, the
                                sea, or the countenance.
Tenuis,   "   ....as that which is thin, slight, or slender.

Inanis,   'vain'............opp. to plenus, and hence empty.
Inritus,   "   ....without method, and hence ineffectual.
Vacuus,   "   ....without influence, as vacua nomina.
Vanus,   "   ....akin to Greek phaino, and hence a mere
                                "will o' the wisp," an ignis fatuus.

Fecundus,   'fertile'........abounding in products.
Felix,   "   ....naturally or constitutionally fruitful
                                in resu'ts.
Ferax,   "   ....inclined by nature to productiveness.
Fertilis,   "   ....produc'ive of fruits or results.
Frugifer,   "   ....fruitbearing, as fields, countries, etc.

Opimus, 'fertile'........as abounding in the best and richest products.

Uber, " ....as r'ch internally, and therefore productive.

Invidus, 'envious'........as unfavorable or unfriendly, bu; not directly hostile.

Lividus, " ....as possessing spiteful or malicious qualities.

Lividulus, " ....as possessing slightly envious qua'ities.

Malignus, " ....as naturally bad in every direction.

Negatives differ much from privatives; nescius is never having known, while inscius is not knowing for the time being.

Nu:lus, 'no one'..........as that wh'ch never did exist.

Nec Ullus, " ....as omi:ting that which does exist.

Nemo, " ....as one that never did exist.

Nul'us non, 'every'.......as an equal to omnis.

Non nullus, 'some'........as an equal to aliquis.

Inanis, 'empty'..........as lacking what might be expected.

Otio‹us, " ....as hands or brains with nothing to do.

Securus, " ....as unconcerned about anything.

Vacuus, " ....as without an inhabitant.

Abundans, 'rich'..........hav:ng more than his barns can hold.

Copiosus, " ....having full barns, larders, and pantries.

Dives, " ....opp. to pauper, and hence lacking nothing.

Ferax, " ....as being fertile.

Fortunatus, " ....having been b'essed by Fortuna.

Lautus, " ....being luxurious.

Locuples, 'rich'...........having much property, particularly in
    lands.

Nummatus, " ....having plenty of money

Opimus, " ....having much that is choice.

Opulentus, " ....having money and influence.

Pecuniosus, " ....having a fulness of money, besides
    being a lover of money.

Pretiosus, " ....being of great value.

Uber, " ....as having within itself an ample suffi-
    ciency.

Altus, 'deep'.............because having reached the limit of
    our greatest measures.

Eruditus, 'deep'..........in the matter of learning

Multus, " ....in consequence of fulness.

Profundus, " ....because the measure is unknown, there
    is no standard as in altus.

Summus, " ....as applied to peace or other abstract
    quality.

Subtilis, " ....as applied to shrewdness.

Fidus, 'true'.............as keeping one's word.

Sincerus, 'true'..........as being genuine.

Germanus, " ....as being born of the same parents.

Verus, " ....as being able to prove itself.

Verax, " ....as always speaking or acting the truth.

Fidelis, " ....as that which can be trusted or relied
    upon.

Doctus, 'learned'........because of having been taught.

Eruditus, " ....because of having been brought out of
    a rude condition by being educated

Litteratus, " ....particularly in the literature of one's
    time.

,...

Abundans, 'full'.......... as it were to overflowing
Affluens, " .... as continually coming, like a stream of water.
Frequens, " .... as coming from all directions.
Plenus, " .... as by occupying all the space within bounds.
Completus, " .... as completely filled.
Oppletus, " .... as filled to the brim wherever the eye can see.
Patulus, " .... as being outspread everywhere.
Confertus, " .... as having material brought together from every quarter.
Refertus, " .... as having been again and again stuffed.
Amicabilis, 'friendly'...... because coming from real friends.
Benevolus, " ...... because always wishing well.
Amicus, " ...... because having the power or disposition to love.
Benignus, " ...... because good natured, born to friendship.
Familiaris, " ...... because like one of the same family.
Humanus, " ...... because having the instincts of men.
Comis, " ...... because companionable.

Cunctus, 'all'.............. as being conjoined, all together.
Integer, 'whole'........... as being unbroken or untouched
Omnis, 'all'............. as every one taken one by one.
Solidus, " .... as compact in one body, Dies solidus.
Totus, " .... as a whole from beginning to end.
Universus, " .... as all turned into one.

Amoenus, 'beautiful'...... because pleasant to the eyes.
Bellus, " ...... because both small and good.
Formosus, " ...... because shapely.
Pulcher, " ...... because fleshy and shapely.
Speciosus, " ...... because of mere appearance.
Venustus, " ...... because made like Venus.

Primus, 'first'............as a natural starting point.
Princeps, " ....as being chief of a band or head of a list, but always with reference to rule or choice.
Primarius, first'..........as among the first in the group.
Procer, " ....as one of the nobles.

Solus, 'alone'.............because by one's self.
Unus solus, 'alone'........because the one has no companion.
Solitarius, " ....because one of a number that has no companions.
Sine arbitris, " ....because without witnesses.
Arbitris remotis, 'alone'...because the witnesses have been removed.

Similis with dative, 'like'..as an external likeness.
Similis, with genitive, 'like.as an internal likeness.
Fatigatus, 'tired'........as having trave ed sufficiently.
Defatigatus, " ....as having repeatedly traveled sufficiently.
Fessus, " ....as having come to the point of being "all broken up."
Lassitudine }
Confectus . } 'tired' ......as being "done for completely" by lassitude.
Lassus. 'tired'............as though muscles could no longer act together.

Antiquus, 'old'..........because belonging to earlier times.
Obsoletus, " ....because having been worn away.
Priscus, " ....because having belonged to former times.
Pristinus, " ....because pertain'ng to the past.
Vetus, " ....because of service in the past.
Veteranus, " ....because pertaining to the past.
Vetustus, " ....because having been used long ago.

Circumdatus,'surrounded by'.as though placed or put in position.
Concretus,   "   " .as having grown together.
Frequens,   "   " .as having come from all directions.
Plenus,   "   " .as filled in on all sides.
Stipatus,   "   " .as though compressed on all sides.

Grandis, 'great'..........as a combination of parts in a body.
Magnus,   " ....as a center of force. The cubic idea, and hence indicative of many sided forcefulness.
Amplus,   " ....as by outspread in at least two directions.
Vastus,   " ....as widespread desolation.
Ingens,   " ....as of something grown to a great size.
Immanis,   " ....as of something unmeasured, enormous.
Spatiosus,   " ....as great by space, linear, square, or cubic.

Beneficus, 'beneficent'.....one who actually does good.
Benignus,   " ......one who was born good; is inherently good.
Liberalis,   " ......one who freely gives of what he has.

Commutabilis, 'changeable'.as one thing capable of being used in many ways.
Diversus,   " .as two or more persons or things of different charac'eristics.
Multiplex,   " .as having many folds or parts.
Mobilis,   " .as one thing easily moved from place to place.
Varius,   " .as one thing having differing forms or features.
Inconstans,   " .as one person or thing not always the same.

Alacer, 'swift'............because qu:ck of wing.

Celer,   "   ....because like birds or winds above the
                            earth

Citus,   "   ....because acting the part of one excited.

Pernix,   "   ....because strugg'ing successfully through
                            difficulties.

Properus, "   ....because hastening to be near.

Rapidus, "   ....because seizing requires rapidity.

Velox,   "   ....because born to "fly."

Volucer,   "   ....because like the bird, always ready to
                            fly.

Salubris, 'healthful'......as bringing or produc!ng health.

Integer,   "   ......as uninjured by harm from any source.

Salutaris, "   ......as tending to healthfulness.

Salutifer, "   ......as transferring healthfulness to us.

Sanus,   "   ......as being sound or well.

Va!idus,   "   ......as having s'rength for a cer!ain purpose.

Salvus,   "   ......as having been preserved.

Firmus,   "   ......as having been propped.

Valens,   "   ......as now strong for some one duty.

Robustus,   "   ......as having the inner, static ability.

Iners,   'slow'............because as seemingly not knowing how
                            to be otherwise.

Piger,   "   ....because d:sinclined, or disabled by
                            reason of inability to put forth ener-
                            gies.

Ignavus, "   ....because inactive by natural physical
                            condition

Lentus,   ."   ....because one muscle is not in harmony
                            with another.

Tardus,   "   ....because one muscle seems to interfere
                            with another.

Serus, 'slow'............because the action was not begun in
time.

Segnis, " ....because always fo'lowing along behind.

Deses, " ....because sitting too much.

Apertus, 'open'..........as that which has been made open.

Patens, " ....as that which is lying open.

Patulus, " ....as 'hat which is widespread.

Propatulus, 'open'.........as having the whole front widespread.

Manifestus, " ....as having been cleared by the hand.

Clarus, " ....as clear, unobscured, and all within
range of vision.

Simplex, " ....as without folds, being outspread before us.

Candidus, " ....as being white and shining by collected
rays.

Opertus, 'covered'........as having been opposed in the act of
opening.

Tectus, " ....by having been roofed over.

Contectus, " ....by having been completely roofed over.

Velatus, " ....by having been veiled.

Protectus, " ....by having been furnished wi'h a roof.

Defensus, " ....by having been guarded against outside foes

Oppletus, " ....by having the objects of sight concealed.

Aequus, 'right'..........as being level.

Fas, " ....as by Divine law.

Justus, " ....as being upright.

Accuratus, " ....as having been done according to care.

Rectus, " ....as being straight.

Verus, " ....as being morally true.

Nativus, 'natural'........arising from nature.

Innatus, " ....as being inborn.

Naturalis, 'natural'.......in accordance with nature's laws.
Insitus, " ....as having been imp.anted.

Aliquis, 'some one'........any one but yourself.
Quivis, " ....any one you wish.
Quis, " ....any one including self.
Quisquis, " ....any one whatsoever.
Ullus, " ....diminutive of unus, and hence any individual.
Qu'libet, " ....any one whom it is pleasing to anybody to name.
Quispiam, " ....any one so far known.

Jejuna, 'poor'............as oratio jejuna.
Exigua, " ....as casa exigua.
Sterilis, " ....as ager sterilis.
Inops, " ....as inops verborum.
Pauper, " ....as opposed to dives.
Tenuis, " ....as having small means.
Mendicus, " ....as a beggar.
Egens, " ....as needing life's nceessaries.
Indigens, " ....as being in absolute want.
Vilis, " ....as being of cheap material.

Diutinus, 'lasting'........as something every day, but not thought of as every moment of the day.
Diuturnus, " ....as something taking in every moment.

Hujusmodi, 'of this kind'...as having been pointed out recent'y or as to be po'nted out immediately.
Ejusmodi, " ...as having been pointed out beforehand.
Talis, " ...as having a measure or standard by which it can be understood.

Par, 'equal'............in linear dimensions.

Aequus, 'equal'...........in surface dimensions.
Quantus, " ....as introducing standards by which their
Qualis, 'equal.'   correlatives may be measured. These
Quot, 'equal.'   always bring in the basis of compar-
Quam, 'equal.'   ison.

Commodus, 'convenient'...as with proper measure.
Opportunus, "   ...as being right at the port or harbor.
Utilis,   "   ...as being serviceable.

Anceps, 'doubtful'........because making nothing decisive.
Dubius,   "   ....because presenting two phases, and yet
                            not permitting a choice.

Alius, 'another'...........as any other except the one named.
Alienus, 'another's'........as belonging to another.
Alter, 'another'...........as one of two persons.

Ceterus,   'rest'..........as all the rest except those mentioned.
Reliquus, "   ....as the remainder after others are gone.

Extremus, 'last'..........either of two ends, the first or last,
                            last or first.
Proximus, "   ....as being nearest to us from either end,
                            but usually to the right side or front.
Postremus, "   ....as opposed to primus, it is last in order.
Ultimus,   "   ....as being farthest from us on either end.
Supremus, "   ....as being highest in the list.

Placidus, 'calm'..........because having been brought to rest, as
                            troubled waters.
Quietus,   "   ....as being asleep.
Tranquillus, "   ....as even more quiet than in sleep
Remissus. "   ....as having been relaxed or brought to
                            rest.

Constans, 'fixed'.......... as being always the same.
Firmus,   "   .... as having been made so by props.
Certus,   "   .... as something already decided and well known.
Stabilis,   "   .... as able to stand by its own gravity.
Intentus,   "   .... as being held in one position: oculi intenti.

Communicans,   'sharing'. as making some one thing common.
Impertiens,   "   . as dividing into parts, giving to two, each a half; to ten, each a tenth, etc.
Partiens,   "   . as simp y giving part, but no fixed par:, to several persons.

Aequales, 'equals'........ because of the same age.
Pares,   "   .... because alike in some one feature.

Egens,   'needy'.......... because wanting the necessaries of life.
Indigens,   "   .... because in absolute want.
Inops,   "   .... because having no resources.

Pauper, 'poor'............ as opposed to dives, as being in reduced circumstances.
Vilis,   "   .... as of small worth, because made of cheap material, or because being out of fashion and not in demand.

Beatus, 'happy'.......... as having been blessed, and hence being satisfied.
Faustus,   "   .... as having been made favorable.
Felix,   "   .... as having everything according to our wishes.
Secundus,   "   .... as results following out efforts, successful.
Fortunatus, "   .... as having been favored by fortune.

Prosperus, 'happy'........as having everything to accord with our hopes.

Acceptus, 'good'..........because the person has been received by the people.

Bonus, " ....because being capable of giving service or he p to others.

Gratus, " ....because pleas'ng to all persons.

Honestus, " ....because honorab e in reali y.

Jucundus, " ....because abounding in good cheer.

Probus, " ....because of having been weighed and not found wanting.

Aeternus, 'eternal'........ the farther continuance of the age (aevum).

Sempiternus, 'eternal'.....the farther continuance of semper.

Ignavus, 'inactive'.........as being without natural energy

Iners, 'inactive'...........as being without skill.

Expletus, 'satisfied'........as having been filled.

Satiatus, 'satisfied'........as having the appetite brought to a standstill.

Dimensus, 'measured'......as by some standard mensura.

Descriptus, " ......as having been laid off by measure.

Dispar, 'different'........because of not the same linear dimensions.

Dissimilis, 'different'......because of not the same form or quality.

Aptus, 'suited'..........as by nature.

Idoneus, " ....as by appearance. Id internal stem of Videre.

Conveniens, " ....as by all the parts harmonizing.

Adverb Terminals.

— e & — o & u . . . . ablative termina'ions and hence indicating cause, manner, means, etc.

— e & — um . . . . neuter singular termina:ions and hence
accusative of specification (?), bet-
ter of generalization.

— im . . . . either an ablative or an accusative
case, and so cause, etc., or case of
specificat'on.

— ter . . . . 'by,' as though an extended form of the
the ablative case and denoting a cus-
tomary action.

— tus (—us) . . . . 'from,' as though an extended form of
the ablat:ve case and denoting the
abstract concept of origin or source
of the action.

(69)

Adverbs.

(255)

Fere, 'almost'........... positive and therefore less close to the number limit.

Ferme, 'almost'.......... superlative and therefore closest to the number limit.

Paene, " .... as the degree, as though getting to some condit'on with pain or difficulty.

Prope, " .... the idea of approximation or approach, nearby.

Propemodum, 'almost'..... often used for prope, and giving modum to show degree.

Post, 'after'.............. for ponst from pone and signifying 'in the rear'

Postea, " .... for post + abl. ea, the latter showing the means

Magis, 'more'............ in degree.

Plus, " .... in quantity.

Melius, 'better'........... in quality.

Potius, 'rather'........... offers a choice.

Clam, 'secretly'........... from celo, 'conceal,' and hence covered up.

Furtim, " .... in the manner of a th'ef.

Occulte, " .... ob + cul=cel, as by concealment before one's eyes.

In occulto, " .... l'teral y in hiding before one's eyes.

Secreto, " .... se + cerno, as by separation.

Aegre, 'scarcely'.......... as though in a sickly manner.

Vix, " .... connected with vis and hence 'with effort.'

Vixdum, " .... strengthened form of vix.

Maxime, 'especially'......as by the use of all force and size.

Potissumum,   "   ......as by the use of all force.

Praecipue,   "   ......as by taking that first and foremost.

Praesertim,   "   ......as by combining that first and fore-
                        most.

Affatim, 'enough'.........as if 'according to fate,' or that which
                        has been spoken.

Satis,   "   ....as that which has come to a standstill.

Aliquantulum, 'little'......a little of some quantity.

Paulum,   "   ......a little in extent of time or space.

Nonnihili,   "   ......in some way, or as in Eng., "in any
                        old way."

Paululum,   "   ......a very little in extent of time or space.

E longinquo, 'afar'........from a distance, as derived from that
                        which is the very beginning or foun-
                        tain head.

Eminus,   "   ....opp. of comminus, literally 'out of
                        hand,' as in fighting by the throwing
                        of darts.

Longe,   "   ....as the position in which anything may
                        be.

Multo,   "   ....as denoting the outspread of time,
                        place or object.

Procul,   "   ....as though so far in front as to be con-
                        cealed from view.

Demum, 'at length'.......the reference is always to some prior
                        state or statement and hense demum
                        is secondary.

Denique,   "   ....always secondary with reference to a
                        primary expressed or understood.

Tandem, 'at length'....... double secondary, and therefore emphatic with reference to something previously said.

Tum, " .... quum is implied as primary, and hence tum is secondary.

Omnino, 'altogether'...... an ablative without a preposition, and hence not restricted to any part of an entirety.

Prorsus, " ...... literally turning (all) forward.

Funditus, " ...... from the very bottom, as in overturning.

Conjunctim, " ...... all joined together, as taking in all kinds and all combinations.

Penitus, " ...... from the inmost recesses.

Plane, " ...... akin to penus, 'full,' and hence fully.

Simul, " ...... at the same time, and hence indicating togetherness with one or more accompaniments.

Una, " ...... from the fact of complete oneness.

Modo, 'lately'............ as by a measure, and hence either long or short. Often used for just now and sometimes a good while ago.

Nuper, " .... fr. novus + per, and hence recently.

Acerbe, 'bitterly'........ as though by sharpness or acridness.

Amare, " .... as though by bitterness to the taste.

Aspere, " .... as though by roughness to the touch.

Vehementer, " .... as though by being driven.

Ita, 'so'.................. in this manner, from same stem as Is, Ea, Id, showing a more special relation than ut.

Hoc modo, 'so'...........in this manner, but limited in the method, and yet emp'oying the who e of the method, if need be.

Hunc in modum, 'so'......in this limited way, but not supposing the whole of the one method to be used.

Sic, 'so'................ always secondary to its primary ut or ita.

Frustra, 'in vain'........disappointed expectation, as though one has been dealt with fraudulently.

(Vir.) Incassum, 'in vain'..into emptiness, into hollowness.

Nequiquam,   "   ..absence of success in effort.

(Liv.) In cassum, "   ..into emptiness.

Irritus,   "   ..withou: thought for the time being, as without a plan.

Nondum, 'not yet'........a relative statement, not ready for a second movement.

Hauddum,   "   ....an absolute statement, not ready for a second movement.

Necdum,   "   ....'and not yet,' a continuous statement, not ready for a second movement

Nequedum,   "   ....'and not yet,' a continuous sta'ement, not ready for a second movement

Adhuc non,   "   ....'up to this time not.'

Ut, 'as'................a real similarity, but without contrast.

Sicut, 'as'...............a real similarity, but with contrast implied.

Quasi, "as'............. a merely conceived sim'larity.

Tamquam, 'as'............a merely conceived similarity, contrast imp'ied.

Velut. 'as'...............in Cic. equal to 'for example;' in late writers, it is used like quasi.

Confestim, 'immediately'... with haste.
Continuo,   "   ....immed'ately after, as moving on together.
Extemplo,   "   ....as out of time, but originating in little time.
Derepente,   "   ....intensive movement, as of serpent.
Instanter,   "   ....as following closely.
Actutum,   "   ....as by the one and same act.
Mature,   "   ....as at the right time.
Illico,   "   ....as in that very place.
Properanter,   "   ....as hastily going on through.
Ilicet,   "   ....as it is now the time to go.
Protinus,   "   ....straight onward as the beginning was made.
Recta,   "   ....as on this straight road, recta via.
Repente,   "   ....present movement of serpent.
Statim,   "   ....without de'ay, without sitting down
Subito,   "   ....suddenly, as though coming up under your feet.

Inconsiderate, 'rash'y'.....without consideration.
Inconsulto,   "   .....without consul'ation.
Fortuito,   "   .....as by chance.
Nimis festinanter, 'rash'y'..w'th too great haste.
Praepropere, 'rashly'.....with undue haste.
Neg'igenter,   "   .....as never making choice.
Stulte,   "   .....as acting the downright fool.
Temere,   "   .....as though blindly.

Gradatim, 'gradually'......as step by s'ep.
Per gradus,   "   ......as through successive steps.
Pede'emptim,   "   ......as by trying 'he way by steps.
Paula'im,   "   ......as 'ittle by litt'e.
Sensim,   "   ......as by perceiving each step.

(?) Imperceptim,
   'gradually'. ....as though no movement could be per-
                    ceived.

Ex parte, 'partly'........from one side only.
Partim,   "   ....as only a part of the whole at one
                    time.
Partite,   "   ....by proper divisions of the whole.

Plerumque, 'frequently'....by spreading over and filling up va-
                    cancies.
Frequenter,   "   ....by coming from different directions in
                    great numbers
Saepe,   "   ....by heaping up as in number of times.
Crebro,   "   ....by growing in size as crowds gathering
                    in numbers.
Saepenumero,   "   ....an emphatic saepe.

Illinc, 'thence'..........from that distant place named before.
Inde,   "   ....from that intermediate place repre-
                    sented by is, ea, id.
Istinc,   "   ....from that place which you occupy.
Abhinc,   "   ....length of time before the present mo-
                    ment.

Antequam, 'before'........as never having been behind.
Priusquam,   "   ....as having been behind, but now being
                    before.
Ante,   "   ....as never having been behind.
Citius,   "   ....as in the manner of one greatly ex-
                    cited.
Prius,   "   ....as having been behind but now being
                    before.

Iterum, 'again'..........a second time.
De integro, "   ....from the entirety, or afresh.

Denuo, 'again'..........from a new position.

Rursus, " ....as turning back over the same road.

Rursum, " ....as turning back over the same road, the lat er being generic, the former specific.

Ubi, 'when'..............as time contrasted with other time, ubi showing the basis of the comparison.

Ut, " ....as a reference to a well-known date.

Cum, " ....as a reference to every time that, i. e.. whenever.

Heri, 'yesterday'..........the day itself as a period of time.

Hesterno die, 'yesterday'...yesterday's day, a period or portion of yesterday.

Adeo, 'so'..............to that degree or point.

Ita, " ....defines more accurate'y than sic.

Ideo, " ....on that account, and suits our therefore.

Sic, " ....always secondary to ut or some primary.

Tam, " ....always secondary to quam expressed or understood.

Tantopere, 'so'..........a.ways secondary to quanto expressed or understood, but used with verbs instead of tam.

In dies, 'daily'............as the days come in, one after another.

In singulos dies, 'daily'....as single days come in, one after another.

Quotidie, 'daily'..........by as many days as come and go, day after day.

Non,	'not'..............	the ordinary or general not.
Ne,	"	used for non in connection with qui-dem.
Haud,	"	an absolute subjective not, generally with adjectives or adverbs.
Haudquaquam,	'not'.....	a stronger expression for haud.
Minus,	"	as being smaller than the required.
Nequaquam,	"	a very general expression for neque.
Neutiquam,	"	similar to nequaquam, but derived from ne + utique.
Minime,	"	the superlative of parvo, and hence 'by the least.'

De improviso,	'suddenly'...	as from the unseen, a secondary concept.
Ex tempore,	"	as not according to the time, as not coming 'out from within the time,' or not part and parcel of the time
Improviso,	" ...	as in any way unforseen, a primary concept, and showing cause, manner means, instrument, etc.
Inopinato,	" ...	as not being even fancied for the time.
Necopinato,	" ...	as not being even fancied at any time
Repente,	" ...	as a creeping movement made by a serpent.
Subito,	" ...	as coming up from beneath,—a snake putting his head out of the grass.

Aliquando,	'once'.........	at some other time, past or future.
Olim,	"	opposed to nunc, the distant past or future.
Quondam,	"	formerly, used of the past only.

Nimis,	'too'............	regular adverb, denoting excess.
Nimium.	"	adjective used as an adverb, and a very general expression.

Nimis multi, 'too many'....as 25 when we need on'y 20.

Nimium saepe, 'too often'..as 25 repetilions when 20 are enough.

Ubi, 'where'............equal cubi, and regular adverbia! form, as an implied contrast with ibi.

Quo,   " ....equal, quo loco, to what place as an implied contrast with eo loco.

Parumper, a little while'..denoting the brief continuance of an action.

Paulisper,   " · " ..denoting a greater continuance.

Benigne, 'yes'............as in offering to perform service kindly.

Immo,   " ....as by the use of the uttermost kindness.

Optime,   " ....as by highest choice.

Quippe,   " ....as giving a reason for the affirmation.

Recte,   " ....as putting the affirmation on correct bases

Dumtaxat, 'only'..........as by making a correct estimate.

Modo,   " ....the common equivilent, and equal to a moderate limit.

Raro,   " ....as to an occasional solitary effort.

Solum,   " ....as by itself, and hence operating alone.

Solummodo, " ....as operating alone and to a limited degree.

Tantum,   " ....as to this extent and no greater.

Tantummodo, 'only'.......as on'y to a limited extent.

Aperte, 'openly'..........as though the object of tru:h were set forth clearly.

Palam,   " ....as though spread out so that all could see.

Publice, 'openly'.........as though not done in a corner.

Alioqui, 'otherwise'.......in some other way, by some other me·hod.

Aliter, " ....in another case.

Secus, " ....as a secondary method, and hence additional.

Forsitan, 'perhaps'........as equal to fors sit an, 'whether there is a chance.'

Fortasse, " ....as if it has taken place by chance.

Jure, 'rightly'............as according to statute law.

Juste, " ....as in the manner of justice.

Recte, " ....as in a straight line and favorably.

Rite, " ....as according to religious ceremonies.

Brevi, 'shortly'..........as in a short time or space

Breviter, " ....as by a brief method or operation.

Al'quando, 'sometimes'....as at some periods in the future.

Interdum, " ....as between times you have opportunity.

Non nunquam, " ....as 'many times' the two negatives increasing the force of the affirmation.

Non jam, 'no longer'......implies that an act or condition has
Nihil jam. gone on to the present time, but is not now operative.

Non diutius, 'no longer'...as of an action or condition that goes no further than the present.

Ex memoria, 'by heart'....as 'out from the memory' by reproduction.

Memoriter, " ....as following the chain of memory, connecting link to link.

Amplius, 'more'..........as extending more widely on both sides.

Magis,   " ....as greater in degree.

Plus,   " ....as extending farther on any side or on all sides.

Identidem, 'likewise'......as of one time like another.

Item,   " ......as in the same manner.

Non semel,   " ......as 'not once,' it is equivalent to several times in the same way.

Plus semel,   " ......as extending beyond one time.

Plus quam semel, 'likewise'. as extending to several times.

Semel et saepius,   " .as once and repeatedly.

Nocte, 'by night'..........as by°the use of any part or all the night.

De nocte,   " ....but for only a part of the night.

Noctu,   " ....as by night after night,' or 'of nights.'

Jam, 'now'..............as having already started a second movement

Modo,   " ....as in time just passed.

Mox,   " ....as in time just future. From moveo, and hence the notion of hereafter.

Nunc,   " ....as the present moment.

Impune, 'with impunity'...as an unpunished person.

Impunite,   " " ...as though by means of exemption from punishment, the word being an ablative.

Impunitus,   " " ...as to the extent of freedom from punishment.

Admodum sero, 'too late'..late to the limit, hence very late.

Nimis sero,   " " ..as undiminished lateness.

Serius,   'too late'..a little late.
Sero,   "   "   ..as by a late action or condition.

Modo, 'just now'..........as in the recent past.
Nuper,   "   ....as in some period last passed.

Certe,   'certainly'........as with fixedness never known to fail.
Profecto,   "   ....as a fact already brought out.
Sane,   "   ....as in a manner peculiar to healthful-
                                ness.
(Plaut,) Opp'do, 'certainly'.as just before the foot, hence clearly
                                visible. .
Immo,   'certainly'........as by this very thing, equal to ipsimo.
Omnino,   "   ....as by every means that could be con-
                                ceived.
Vere,   "   ....as in a true manner.
Vero,   "   ....as by the truth.
Verum,   "   ....as the truth itself
Quidem,   "   ....perhaps more conjunction than adverb,
                                but used as a strengthener for other
                                adverbs.
Videlicet,   "   ....as giving permission to see for your-
                                self.
Saltem,   "   ....as from salus, representing the idea of
                                healthfu'ly.
Scilicet,   "   ....as giving permission to know how it
                                was done.

Multo minus, 'much less'..as by a much smaller measure.
Nedum,   "   "   ..as 'while not' considering the present
                                or other times and conditions.

Parum,   'little'..........opposed to satis and nimium, from
                                same root as parvus.
Parvum.   "   ....opposed to magnus, and hence little in
                                cubic dimensions.

Paulum, 'little'........... as the extent of time, or as the degree of difference.

Diu, 'for a long time'...... an old ablative of dies, and hence denoting length of time.

Jam diu, " " ...... already a long time.

Longe, " " ...... as by length of days or years.

Jam dudum,'for a long time'.already for a long time, dudum equal diu and dum.

Jam pridem, " " .already a long time before.

Etiam, 'also'............. always adds a new circumstance.

Quoque, " .... denotes the addition of a thing of similar kind.

Vel, " .... when used alone with superlatives.

Umquam, 'ever'.......... as at any one time.

Semper, " .... as being the same all the time.

Ubique, 'everywhere'...... at any one place.

Undique, " ...... from every place.

Passim, " ...... as scattered here and there.

A fronte, 'front'.......... as from the front of your own line and upon the front of your enemy's line.

In fronte, " .... as in the front of your enemy's line.

Adhuc, 'hitherto'......... all the time up to the present time.

Hactenus, " .... all the space or circumstances up to this point.

in equo, 'horseback'...... on the horse, as simply in position.

Ex equo, " ...... from the horse, as performing an action with reference to something different from the horse.

Ut, 'how'...............as expressive of position, ut me cir-
cumsteterint.

Utcumque, 'how'.........'howsoever,' as the most general manner in action.

Quam,   "   ....as an exclamatory modifier of adjectives.

Qui,   "   ....an ancient ablative singular for all
genders.

Quanto,   "   ....as the standard of quantitative measure.

Quem ad modum, 'how'....as 'according to some measure' setting
forth an actual occurrence.

Quo modo, 'how'.........as by some limited simple measure.

Quo pacto, "   ....as by some agreement already made,
and to be lived up to by both parties.

Invite, 'involuntarily'......as not forcefully, but sluggishly,
and always modifying the verb.

Invitus,   "   ......but always modifies subject.

Haud sponte sua,
'involuntarily' ....as not according to one's promise, or
better perhaps, 'not by promise,' but
because some one insists.

Nolens, 'involuntarily'.....as not being a willing performance.

Orto,   "   .....as by impulse and not will.

Ultro, 'voluntarily'........by some way outside of the ordinary.
not being required by one's sur-
roundings.

Sua sponte, 'voluntarily'...as by one's own promise.

Facto,   "   ...as by determination and purpose already formed.

Volens,   "   ...as being a willing performance.

(?) Infrequenter, 'rarely'..as not coming in numbers.

Raro, 'rarely'............as being only here and there, and so
seldom met with.

Quamvis, 'however'.......as far as you may wish to go.
Quamlibet, " ....as far as anybody may wish to go.

Nunquam non, 'never not'.. litotes for 'at all times.'
Non nunquam, 'not never'.. litotes for 'sometimes.'

Difference of Terminals
for Nouns.
(1) From Verbs.

—or ....the man who performs the action implied in the verb.
—tor ....those that end in —tor form feminines
in —trix.
—sor ....those that end in —sor form feminines
in —trix or —strix, sometimes throw-
ing out the L of the mas, and then
adding —trix.
The termination or, when added to
the unaltered stem of the verb, especially of intransitive verbs, expresses
the action or condition of the verb
as a substantive, as **favor, furor,**
n'tor, etc.
There is much difference be'ween
—or and —er in English. Or de-
no'es profess!onal cont'nuance, while
—er represents temporary or occasional emp'oyment.
—io ....when added to the supine after the
—us. loss of um, express the action or condition denoted by the verb abstract-
ly. —io continuously, —us fixedly.

—ura .... has nearly the same meaning as —us.

—ela .... has nearly the same meaning as —ura. Both these terminals denote simple extension of the original.

—men .... expresses either the thing to which the action belongs, both in an active and passive sense, or the means of attaining what the verb expresses.

—mentum .... the means of attaining what the verb expresses.

—bulum .... denote an instrument or place serving
—culum.   a certain purpose in connection with the verb, culum being sometimes contracted into —clum and then —clum changing into crum.

—trum .... carries about the same meaning as —clum.

—a .... when appended to the stem of a verb,
—o.   denote the subject of the action.

—io .... when appended to the stems of substantives, the new nouns express the idea of the trade to which a person belongs.

—ium .... expresses the general effect of the verb and the place of the action.

—igo .... expresses a state or condition.

—ido .... expresses a state or condition.

(2) From Substantives.

—ellus, —ella, —ellum... appended only in words of first and second dec., which have e, ra, or an r in their terminations.

—ulus, —ula, —ulum,   mean little, and are appended to the
—culus, —cula, —culum.   stem after the removal of the termination of the oblique cases.

—olus, —ola, —olum..... are used when the termination of the primitive substantive is preceded by a vowel

—illus, —illa, —illum.... more rare than the other forms for diminutives.

—unculus, a, um........ puts un for on as found in words like sermo, ratio, etc

—ium .... appended to noun-stems, it expresses an assemblage. When appended to verbal substantives in or, it denotes the place where.

—arium .... denotes a receptace.

—etum .... appended to the names of plants, denotes the place where they grow in great number.

—ie .... appended to names of animals, indicates the place in which they are kept.

—ides .... terminals belonging to masculine pat-
—as. ronymics, but both s and des are sim-
—iades. plv secondary signs, the primary being given by the original name.

—is .... feminine terminal for secondaries.
S in Jones, Marks, etc., and s in all p'urals in English and many other languages is simply the sign of the secondary extension of the primary concept.

(3) From Adjectives.

—itas .... denotes the quality expressed by the adjective. Adjectives in —ius make substant'ves in —ietas; those in stus make them in stas.

—ia .... abstract notion of the quality expressed
—itis. by the adjective.
—tudo .... denotes greater duration in quality than
—itas.
—edo .... found in only few words.
—monia .... abstract notion of quality; and like
—tudo denotes duration and pecul-
iarity of the quali.y more than —ela.
Hence querimonia is a stronger term
than quereia.

(152)
Nouns.
(709)

Acies, 'army'............the battle line drawn up in form of a
wedge.
Agmen, " ....the army on the march.
Copiae, " ....troops in the collective capacity.
Exercitus, " ....the army that has been drilled.
Milites, " ....the individual soldiers.
Vires, " ....forces as dynamic or effective powers.

Epstula, 'letter'..........as writing sent to some one.
Litera, " ....as a letter of the alphabet.
Literae, " ....as something written.

Literae, 'learning'........as knowledge expressed in writing.
Doctrina, " ....as knowledge taught.
Eruditio, " ....as the means of mental and moral cul-
ture.
Humanitas, " ....as the refinement of education and
taste.

Cognitio, 'knowledge'......subjective or static knowledge.

Notitia, 'knowledge'....... general knowledge—all knowledge.
Scientia,   "   ...... practical knowledge, illustrated in the
world about us.

Certamen, 'fight'.......... the effort to decide the contest in favor
of either party.
Pugilatio,   "   .... the action of fighting, fight in progress.
Pugilatus,   "   .... the finished fight.
Pugna,   "   .... general term for any kind of fight.
Proelium,   "   .... general term for a fight with arms.
Dimicatio,   "   .... actual battle in progress, arms gleam-
ing on both sides.

Caput, 'chief'............ as the most important person or thing
in any line of thinking.
Primus,   "   .... as the first in time or order.
Princeps,   "   .... as the foremost whom others follow.
Praefectus, 'chief'........ as having been made superintendent or
temporary governor.
Principes, 'chiefs'........ as leading men in the state or com-
munity.
Proceres,   "   .... as nobles or princes of the realm.

Liber, 'free'............ a man born free,—generosus is better.
Libertus, "   .... one freed by h's master.
Libertinus, 'free'.......... one socially and politically free.
The distinction be'ween libertus
and libertinus is largely abandoned
in post-Augustan Latin

Dies, 'day'.............. sing. fem often means a period of time;
sing mas. usually 24 hours.
Dies, 'days'............ pl. mas., as always in pl., 24 hour periods.

Talos, 'dice'..............four flat and two round sides.
Tessaras, 'dice'...........six flat sides.

Auxilium, 'help'..........fr. augere, hence what increases our
                        strength.
Subsidium, " ....aid near at hand and ready to be given.
Adjumentum, 'help'.......the means of help.
Opera, 'help'..,..........by actual effort.
Praesidium, 'he'p'.........as a shield from attack.
Suppetiae, 'help'..........present help of troops.

Deos, 'gods'.............:...nature gods
Divos, " ....demigods or deified emperors.
Lares, " ....tutelary gods.
Penates, 'gods'...........those gods that preside over the larder
                        and provide food for the home.
Numen,   " ....the divinity of the godhead, literally the
                        nod or authority of a god.

Poena, 'punishment'......originally fine paid for murder, later
                        any punishment.
Supplicium, 'punishment'..begging for pardon in the presence of
                        the executioner.
Animadversio,   " ..censure, but used euphemistically for
                        capital punishment.
Castigatio,   " ..as that which purifies or benefits.
Damnum,   " ..as by loss or injury.
Multa,   " ..originally a fine in cattle, later in
                        money.
Multatio,   " ..the action of fining.
Noxa,   " ..as by the effect of injury.

Raptor, 'robber'..........one who takes by force anything he
                        may desire. The general term.

Ereptor, 'robber'..........the plunderer in large measure of goods
or of liberty.

Direptor, " ....pillager of the secondary class

Fur, 'thief'..............as one who takes any and every kind
of thing he may desire.

Latro, 'robber'...........one who lies in concealment.

Pirata, " ....p'rate, one who makes attacks on ships.

Praedo, " ....one who seeks booty of any kind.

Amnis, 'river'............as a generic, often used for the larger
streams.

Flumen, 'river'..........any considerable flow of water.

Fluvius, " ....as the contrad'stinction to noisy bodies
of wa'er.

Torrens, " ....as steaming, rush'ng, boiling water.

Rivus, " ....as a brook or small stream of water
or other fluids.

Rivulus, " ....rather a brooklet.

Amentia, 'madness'.......as a primary idea, and hence general
and comp'ete.

Dementia, ". ....as a secondary idea, and hence specific
and partial.

Furor, " ....as that ispired by the Furies.

Insania, " ....as due to unsoundness, an excessive
action of any faculty or appetite.

Rabies, " ....as due to disease which has, as it were
seized upon us.

Vecordia, " ....as due to senselessness.

Dom'natio, 'power'........as arb'trary or tyrannical government.

Dicio, • " ....as authority due to terms of surrender.

Facultas, " ....as the means of doing something.

Imperium, " ....as military command.

Potentia, 'power'..........as actual and effective.

Potestas, " ....as standing power over persons or nations.

Regnum, " ....as kingly government.

Robur, " ....as sta.ic or internal strength.

Vis, " ....as dynamic or available power.

Homo, 'man'.............as a human being, often used contemptuously.

Vir, " ....as a man in contradistinction to woman, as a hero with the dynamic vis visible in all his actions.

Senectus, 'old age'........the state of a person who has passed through the other five stages of life.

Senium, " ....in its weakness without any special thought of the successions.

Jusjurandum, 'oath'.......as one taken before the law courts.

Sacramentum, " ....as one administered to soldiers when they were enlisted.

Gens, 'nation'............as taken by families.

Natio, ' " ....as taken by descent from original families.

Populus, " ....as the political whole.

Aes, 'money'.............as copper, the basis of estimation.

Argentum, 'money'........as silver coin.

Nummus, " ....the regular silver currency, and as a sesterce about 4½ cents.

Pecunia, " ....as wealth, so called because the Roman's wealth consisted origina ly of cattle.

Custodia, 'guard'.........as the action or condition of custos or
          custodes.
Custodes,   " ....as keepers of whatever may be en-
          trusted to them.
Excubiae,   " ....as the action or condition of those
          who lie out of doors.
Excubitores, " ....as actual out of door guards.
Praesidium, 'guard'.......as an army just outside the city walls.
Speculatores, " ....as those persons who are watching
          from towers.
Statio,   " ....as a picket guard on the outposts.
Vigilae,   " ....as the action or condition of those
          awake.
Vigiles,   " ....as persons who are really awake.
Vinculum,   " ....as a bolt for a door

Dedecus, 'shame'.........as what is unbecoming any reasonable
          being.
Flagitium,   " ....as a crime committed in the heat of
          passion.
Infamia,   " ....as disgraceful and notorious.
Ignominia,   " ....as the deprivation of one's good name.
Libio,   " ....as the act of a mere animal nature.
Pudicitia,   " ....shamefacedness or modesty.
Pudor,   " ....the feeling of shame that comes to a
          pure nature.
Probrum,   " ....any shameful, infamous deed.
Stuprum,   " ....opp. of pudicitia in the sense of im-
          modesty.
Turpitudo,   " ....baseness belonging to low birth, as a
          condition common to the Turba.

Animus, 'mind'.........the whole inner self, both mind and
          heart.

Genius,   'mind'.........simp'y inborn ability.

Ingenium,   " ....the inborn ability for outer productive-
                    ness.

Mens,   " ....the power of thinking.

Anima,   'life'...........the basis for both spiritus and vita.

Spiritus,   " ....the ou.er proof of inner anima.

Vita,   " ....the outer proof of both anima and
                    animus, as connected with vis and
                    vir.

Orbis terrarum, 'earth'....as the entire circle of lands.

Tellus, 'earth'...........the globe as to all its limitations.

Terra,   " ....the land as distinguished from the
                    wa.er.

Solum,   " ....the land as the productive portion of
                    earth, or as what we call soil.

Ager, 'territory'..........as that which may be cultivated.

Colonia,   " ....as that into which colonists are sent.

Fines,   " ....as the imaginary boundar'es of land.

Regio,   " ....as any district wi'h distinct boundaries.

Terra,   " ....as land in its widest sense.

Territorium, 'territory'.....as the land that belongs to a town or
                    district of the country.

Compos, 'master'.........as having control of one's own powers.

Dominus,   " ....as a master or owner.

Dynastes,   " ....as a ruler or prince.

Herus,   " ....as the head of a household.

Magister,   " ....as a very general term for any one
                    great enough for command.

Paterfamilias, 'master'....as the head of both children and slaves,
                    and the manager of business.

Princeps,	"	....as the first man in the state.
Tyrannus,	"	....as a ruler in the most absolute sense.

Ancilla,	'servant'.........	as a waiting-maid.
Verna,	"	as one born in the house, not bought.
Assecla,	"	as one who follows, a mere sycophant. The word being used in a contemptuous sense.
Famulus,	"	as one who serves, being part of familia.
Mancipium,	"	as a slave that has been bought.
Minister,	"	as a helper in any business.
Puer,	"	as a young roustabout.
Servus,	"	as one bound for life and without politica. standing.

Baculum,	'staff'..........	the cane on which one leans in walking.
Bacillum,	"	a little staff or the lictor's staff.
Caduceus,	"	a herald's staff, as was Mercury's.
Clava,	"	a knotty staff or cudgel, as was that of Hercules.
Fustis,	" ..:.......	the ordinary club or cudgel.
Hastile,	"	staff of a spear, and sometimes the spear itself.
Lituus,	"	augur's staff, which was curved; and hence the word is sometimes used for a clarion or curved trumpet.
Palus,	"	as a stake on which Roman recruits exercised their weapons.
Pedum,	"	shepherd's staff.
Scipio,	"	carried before officials, as was the scipio eburneus carried in triumphal procession.

Debïtum,   'duty'..........as a debt due to any one.

Munus,   "   ....as a performance or function.

Officium,   "   ....as the whole body of one's duties.

Locus,   "   ....duty appointed.

Partes,   "   ....the particular part or parts of service
                            any one may have had alloted to him.

Pietas,   "   ....filial duty, as to parents, country, or
                            the gods.

Provincia,   "   ....duty imposed upon us.

Religio,   "   ....as that performed in obedience to con-
                            science.

Sors,   " · ....duty given by lot.

Acies,   'sight'............as the piercing power of the eye.

Oculus,   "   ....as the whole power of the eye.

Visio,   "   ....as the distinguishing power of the eye.

Visus,   "   ....as the image already formed on the
                             retina.

Videndi facultas, 'sight'... as the simple power of performing the
                             function of securing an image.

Capillus, 'hair'..........of the head. Pilus is a single hair.

Coma,   "   ....of the head, but loose and flowing; of-
                            ten used of the beard and of the tail
                            of the comet and of the foliage of
                            trees, etc.

Crinis,   "   ....hair in bunches and bushy.

Adjutor, 'helper'.........but not an inferior, usually one selected
                           as fully competent by experience.

Adjutrix,   "   ....a fema'e helper, but not a servant.

Minister,   "   ....as an inferior the min being the same
                           stem as found in minus.

Conjugium, 'marriage'.... as the union of husband and wife.

Connubium, " .... as the veiling of the wife for marriage.

Matrimonium, " .... as the state of a married woman.

Nuptiae, " .... as all the preparations and ceremonies connected with the marriage.

Jus Connubii, " .... as the legal privilege of marriage.

Procella, 'storm'.......... as that which is driving forward.

Tempestas, 'storm'........ as immoderate weather conditions.

Turbo, " .... as a whirlwind in its fury.

Gradus, 'step'............ as any single movement of the foot up or down or forward or backward.

Gressus, " .... as continuous walking.

Passus, " .... as the measure of a step, but what the Roman called a passus as a measure in length was really two full steps, making five feet.

Effigies, 'likeness'........ that which brings the within or the hidden outward.

Forma, " .... that which represents the outline of an object.

Imago, " .... a likeness which reveals all the features

Figura, ' ' " .... simply the external shape.

Instar, " .... as the equal of an object.

Picta, " .... as that which is painted.

Pictura, " .... the surface form of a painting.

Similitudo, " .... the apparent sameness of features.

Signum, " . ... especially of the gods, but often representing as a symbol what cannot be represented in any form.

Simulacrum, 'likeness'..... but only an imperfect representation, as the statue of a god.

Statua, " ..... the image of a man as set up in a public place.

Tabula, " ..... as a panel on which there is a painting.

Aspectus, 'view'.......... limit of vision, power of vision, or
                                   mere appearance.

Conspectus, 'view'........ our full sight of anything physical or
                                   mental.

Despectus,   "   .... a downward view upon anything ma-
                                   terial or moral.

Prospectus,   "   .... our outlook upon anything in the dis-
                                   tance.

Oppugnatio, 'siege'........ as a most furious storming of fort or
                                   city.

Obsessio,   "   .... as the present act of a siege.

Obsidium,   "   .... the general term for the condition of
                                   a siege.

Obsidio,   "   .... the active operation of a siege in any
                                   or all its details.

Aegritudo, 'sickness'...... state or condition of body or mind.

Aegrotatio,   "   ...... continuance of any disaffection of
                                   body or mind.

Contagio,   "   ...... cause of disease, as by contact with
                                   persons.

Lues,   "   ...... as a plague widespread, and hence af-
                                   fecting many.

Morbus,   "   ...... specific disease, the word being general
                                   for any one form of disease.

Pestilentia,   "   ...... an infectious rather than a contagious
                                   disease.

Valetudo,   "   ...... a state of ill-health rather than real
                                   sickness.

Vomitus,   " .   ... as that which proves revulsion of the
                                   stomach to any of its contents.

Ager, 'country'.......... cultivated or open land as opposed to
                                   the city.

Patria, 'country'.........our fatherland.
Regio, " ....as that which is under control.
Rus, " ....as simply out of town.

Conscientia, 'conscience'...as a consciousness of right and wrong.
Fides, " ...as the keeping of one's word
Religio, " ...as a conscientiousness of one's duty or responsibility.

Finis, "boundary".......from findo, 'cut,' and hence the imaginary line between countries or any boundary be:ween things that are to be distinguished from one another.
Limes, " ....a secondary to finis, and indicating a section line rather than the outside boundary.
Terminus, " ....may represent a real line, but is rather the stone set up as a boundary corner.

Granum, 'grain'..........a grain or seed of any plant.
Frumentum, 'grain'.......harvested grain.
Frumenta, 'grains'.......on the stalk.
Annonae, " ....yearly crop of grain.

Donum, 'gift'............what is given as a mere present, no particular merit or service considered.
Munus, " ....as an affectionate service or favor.
Praemium, 'gift'..........as a reward of merit.

Amitinus, 'cousin'........a child of a mother's brother or a father's sister.
Consobrini, 'cousins'......children of sisters.
Patrueles, " ....children of brothers.
Sobrini, " ....children of consobrini, second cousins.

Area,	'place'	open p!ace not occupied with buildings, field in middle of town.
Campus,	"	free, open place, but larger than an area.
Locus,	"	position which something occupies.
Propatulum,	'place'	in front of a dwelling house, open and unroofed.
Pagus,	"	a village or district, the boundaries of which have been agreed upon.
Regio,	"	a district under governmental control.
Vestibulum,	"	entrance court to home or temple or sepulcher or other place which has larger space.
Vicus,	"	a village as a quarter of town or city.
Sedes,	"	natural position or seat for person, bui!ding, etc.

Spat:um,	'space'	Dorian spadion for stadion (?), extension in length and breadth, spat by prosthesis for pat in pateo, 'extend.'
Curriculum,	'space'	space for a race.

Crimen,	'charge'	of crime, crimination or accusation.
Delictum,	'crime'	properly a delinquency or failure to perform one's obligations.
Facinus,	"	any deed, good or bad, but generally used for a villainy.
Flagitium,	"	shameful, disgraceful crime against morals, and therefore punished by some nations secretly.
Maleficium,	"	a general term for any wrong action.
Nefas,	"	a crime against the laws of the gods.
Scelus,	"	an infamous crime, as of that committed against the laws of one's country.

Consuetudo, 'custom'......as that to which we have been long accustomed, and hence as something well established.

Institutum, " ......as having been established, but more local and peculiar in character.

Mos, " ......as the will or wish of individuals expressing their preference for this or that fashion in speech or manner of life

Usus, " ......as the practice of individuals or the experience of one or many.

Exitus, 'death'..........as the going out from home or off the stage, and hence as an absence from the scene of former activity.

Finis, " ...,......as the boundary between the present and future.

Interitus, " ....as the destruction, or annihilation of persons and things.

Letum, " ....death as a blotting out, fr. lere, 'to destroy.

Mors, " ....as from natural causes.

Nex, " ....violent death as a penalty.

Obitus, " ....as a departure in the sense not of going out of a house, but of meeting an enemy or of going down, as the sun.

Cura, 'care'..............opp to negligentia, and hence living and acting with consideration of all duties and responsibilities.

Diligentia, 'care'..........with respect to one or more objects that require choice of attention.

Sollicitudo, 'care'.........as anxiety with regard to any person or thing that is of interest to us.

Prudentia, " ....as wise foresight.

Conatus, 'effort'......... use of all one's powers in doing any-
                                                 thing.
Industria,   "   .... persistent effort.
Contentio,   "   .... effort in speaking.
Labor,   "   .... effort attended with difficulty.
Pensum,   "   .... a task, as something weighed out.
Opera,   "   .... an effort in any direction.
Opus,   "   .... finished work, as a book.
Studium,   "   .... fixedness of purpose in pursuit.
Nisus,   "   .... struggle as that of an athlete.

Digressio, 'going away'.... the action in progress.
Digressus,   "   "   .... a finished action, a digression already
                                                 made.
Discessio,   "   "   .... the action in progress.
Discessus,   "   "   .... a finished action, a separation already
                                                 made.

Amiculum, 'garment'...... as a cloak or mantle, by which any-
                                                 thing may be covered.
Vestis,   "   ...... the clothing, any article of clothing.
Vestimentum, "   ...... one garment.
Vestitus,   "   ...... everything in the way of clothes.

Gens, 'stock'............ several families connected by birth.
Genus,   "   .... as descendant of any one family.
Stirps,   "   .... as the original head of the family.

Ardor, 'fire'.............. as a general term for whatever exhibits
                                                 the inner heat of actual fire or zeal
                                                 or love.
Flamma, 'fire'............ as the blaze which spreads itself.
Ignis,   "   .... as rather the essence of all heat.
Incendium; 'fire'......... as a conflagration that has been started
                                                 from the outside of building or other
                                                 body.
Scintillae,   "   .... as the sparks that fly off, faint traces

Existimatio, 'opinion'......as an estimation still in progress.

Opinio, " ......as the way in which one sees anything.

Dogma, " ......as a philosophical fact that has been taught.

Decretum, " ......as a principle discovered or that has grown out of facts already established.

Judicium, " ......as according to power of judgment.

Sententia, " ......as one has perceived relations.

Praeceptum, " ......as a precept worthy to be received from a teacher.

Conventio, 'treaty'........action of agreement, but not binding by law.

Conventus, " ....finished act of agreement, but not binding·by law.

Foedus, " ....alliance sanctioned by senate and peop'e.

Pactio, " ········ the making of a legal contract between contending parties.

Pactum, " ....the legal contract between contending part'es.

Sponsio, " ....the action of two generals looking to ratification, but not yet ratified by the states which the generals represent.

Caterva, 'band'..........as a crowd or troop; company of actors; chorus

Cohors, " ....as the tenth part of a Roman legion.

Globus, " ....as a mass of people, or as any large globe.

Grex, " ....more limited than globus; often an association.

Manus, " ....any body of men act'ng together, as hands in the accomplishment of service.

Adversarius, 'enemy' ...... at law, as one who meets us on any one issue, his way or method opposed to ours.

Hostis, " ...... a public enemy, originally a stranger, and hence one having little regard for our interests.

Inimicus, " ...... a private enemy, as being hostile or harmful to us or to our highest good.

Acinaces, 'sword' .... Persian sword, short, but having two edges.

Ensis, " .... a long sword for fighting at a distance.

Gladius, " .... a short sword for fighting close at hand.

Mucro, " .... as the sharp point of any weapon.

Hasta, 'dart' .... a spear for piercing or hurling by hand and with strap attached to bring it back.

Jaculum, 'dart' .... a dart to be thrown, but not with expectation of its return.

Pilum, " .... a short javelin for the infantry.

Telum, " .... a dart for offensive warfare, which may be thrown against the enemy at any reasonab'e distance.

Tragula, " .... seems to have been used to strike and then drag.

Verutum, " .... but more like hasta, from its piercing effects.

Servitium, 'slavery' .... as the service which a slave performs.

Servitudo, " .... as the s ate in which a slave is

Servitus, " .... as the fact or realization of one who has been made a slave.

Cervix, 'neck' .... as the back part of the neck.

Collum, 'neck'............as the entire connection of head and body.

Fauces, " ....as the passway through the neck.

Gula, " ....as the tube or the solid part around the passway.

Patientia, 'endurance'.....as a condition of body or mind or sp'rit.

Perpessio, " .....as the present feeling of dolorum or laborum.

Tolerantia, " .....as the condition of body or mind or spirit from the taking upon ourselves burdens.

Toleratio, " .....as the capacity for bearing the burdens.

Cautes, 'rock'...........rock to be avoided, fr. cavere, 'beware.'

Rupes, " ....steep, broken rock, fr. rumpere, 'break.'

Saxum, " ....any mass of stones detached from cliffs.

Scopulus, " ....dangerous rocks in the water, c'iff.

Silex, " ....hard, flinty granite or basalt.

Consp'ratores, 'conspirators'.those in the business of do'ng secret work against the government.

Conjurati, . . . "......those who have sworn to do violence against government or its officia's.

Dux, 'general'............as a leader of bands.

Imperator, 'general'.......as a commander with authority.

Iter, 'road'.............a route through the coun'ry, but not a prepared via.

Semita, 'road'...........as only a foot path.

Via, " ....as a main road or thoroughfare through the city or country.

Daps, 'feast'..............the sacrificial feast or an expensive feast.

Convivium, 'feast'........the being together, the enjoyment of society, with eating and drinking as a secondary consideration.

Epulae, " ....the actual banquet, with the eating and drinking as a primary consideration.

Epulum, " ....as a solemn or public banquet.

Coena, " ....as the chief meal of the Romans, which was taken after the business of the day

Gaudium, 'joy'...........subjective or static joy.

Dulcedo, " ....sweetness of anything that pleases.

Laetitia, " ....the expression of joy.

Luxuria, " ....the joy that belongs to reveling.

Delectatio, " ....the action of joy,—joy in progress.

Deliciae, " ....the object of joy.

Oblectatio, " ....primary, and therefore generic joy.

Voluptas, " ....the sensation of joy.

Hilaritas, " ....abounding joy as shown in expression or action.

Suavitas, " ....agreeableness to the taste

Otium, 'rest'............(opp. of negotium), rest from outside business.

Pax, " ....absence of any conflict.

Quies, " ....absence of activity, often for sleep.

Requies, " ....refreshing rest, re representing continuance or abundance of rest.

Tranquillitas, 'rest'........undisturbed rest.

Animus, 'courage'........as the spirit of greatness.

Audacia, " ....as the eagerness with which we undertake good or bad service.

Ferocia, " ....as the disposition of the wild beast.

Fortitudo, 'courage'.......as the state of one who bears much.
Temeritas, " ....courage that runs to fool-hardiness.
Virtus, " ....outer proof of inner worth.

Delator, 'informer'........who carried to the authorities all he learned.
Index, " ....as one who points out or discloses as far as he knows persons or places to be watched.
Inquisitor, " ....one who makes it his business to search out everything that may seem hostile to the ruler or the government.

Mundus, 'world'..........as the Greek kosmos, the orderly arrangement of all the universe.
Rerum Natura, 'world'....as the natural state of all things.
Orbis, " ....as the circular form of the world
Terrae, " ....as the dry land of all the world.

Tempestas, 'time'........season, as spring, summer, etc.
Tempus, " ....any length of time.

Commodum, 'gain'........as an advantage just to suit.
Compendium, 'ga'n'......as savings.
Emolumentum, " ......opp. of detrimentum.
Fructus, " ......as natural grow'h.
Lucrum, " ......opp. to damnum.
Merces, " ......as by wages.
Praeda, " ......as by booty.
Praemium, " ......as a pr'ze.
Pret'um, " ......as by va'ues.
Quaestus, " ......as by profit.

Appellatio, 'name'........the tit'e or what somebody calls you.
Nomen, " ....fr. noscere, 'know,' and hence what is well known. Your real name.

Lucus, 'grove'............ sacred grove, consecrated wood.

Nemus,　　"　 .... a wood with glades and pasture lands for horses and catt.e.

Dignitas, 'worthiness'..... as a condition fit to receive all that is best.

Honestas,　　"　 ..... as a state resulting from the office one holds.

Integritas,　　"　 ..... as completeness of character.

Praestantia,　　"　 ..... as pre-eminence from numerous virtues.

Formido,　 'fear'.......... the fear that makes the hair stand up as stubb e in a harvest field.

Horror,　　"　 .... the fear that mekes one shake.

Ignavia,　　"　 .... inborn cowardice.

Metus,　　"　 .... mental fear arising from foresight.

Pallor,　　"　 .... whiteness of the face from sudden fear.

Pavor,　　"　 .... arising from loss of hope or resources.

Terror,　　"　 .... the fear that seems to dry up one's blood.

Timor,　　"　 .... bodily fear from danger immediately before us.

Trepidatio,　"　 .... the trembling fear that causes restless movements.

Verecundia, 'fear'........ as reverence causing modesty, humility or bashfu'ness.

Aedes sacra, 'temple'...... as the sacred house of some god.

Aedicula.　　"　 ...... as a small building, the temple of a god abstractly considered as that of victory.

De'ubrum,　　"　 ...... as the place for expiatory sacrifices.

Fanum,　　"　 ...... as the place where oracles may be given out by the god who inhabits the tem-p'e.

Sacrarium, 'temple'.........as the place where sacred things are kept.

Sacellum, " ......as a small shrine or place consecrated to some deity.

Templum, " ......as the place dedicated to a particular deity.

Fas, 'right'..............as in the sight of the gods.

Aequitas, 'right'..........a quality inherent in a person or thing.

Jus, " ....as common to humanity, both natural and divine.

Justitia, " ....the virtue itself and the love of it.

Lex, " ....the written law as opposed to customs.

Nefas, 'wrong'...........as always wrong, because wrong in the sight of the gods.

Damnum, " ....as injury or loss, being given as a punishment.

Injuria, " ....as contrary to both natural and divine law.

Iniquitas, " ....as contrary to reason, absolute unfairness.

Culpa, 'fault'............fault of the will.

Vitium, " ....fault of the nature.

Arrogantia, 'pride'........bad pride, assumption.

Contumacia, " ....puffed up pride.

Fastidium, " ....contempt-dealing pride.

Fastus, " ....scorn-showing pride.

Insolentia, " ....extraordinary pride, insolence.

Spiritus, " ....high spirit, inner pride that shows in acting the superior toward others

Superbia, " ....haughtiness which says, "I am superior."

Auctor, 'teacher'.........inventor or founder of some system.

Doctor, "   ....one who has been taught.

Explicator, " ....one who unfolds some system.

Expositor, " ....one who sets forth the principles of a system.

Instructor, " ....one who builds up his students on princip:es.

Magister, " ....one who is a leader or director in education.

Praeceptor, " ....one who teaches beforehand arts worthy to be used.

Professor, " ....a public teacher,—late Latin.

Maceria, 'wall'...........wall of clay, etc., around gardens, vineyards, etc.

Moenia, " ....of a city for defence.

Murus, " ....general name for outside wall.

Paries, "..........partition in a building or between houses.

Parietinae, " ....ruins of old houses.

Propugnacula, 'wall'.......wals for keeping the enemy away from murus.

Societas, 'friendship'......association or business that is common, but not home

Communitas, 'friendship'...a closer relationship than societas requires, but still home is not common.

Familiaritas, " ..friendship like that of the fami'y, but each member claiming certain things as his own.

Amicitia, " ..relationship in which all property rights are common. The Greek proverb had it amicorum esse communia omnia.

Comitatus, " ..as companionship in travel.

Ars,   'rule'............as a theory to be tested.

Lex,   "   ....as a written law for conduct.

Modus, "   ....as a method of procedure.

Norma, "   ....originally the carpenter's square for measuring angles, and hence an accurate rule.

Praeceptum, 'rule'........a rule announced beforehand, so that action may be reasonably correct.

Praescriptum, "   ....a rule written beforehand, so that action may be in accord with the rule.

Ratio,   "   ....a general term for any kind of method, manner or way, by which anything may be done.

Regula,   "   ....originally any straight stick, by which exact lines could be drawn.

Ales, 'bird'.............bird bcause of its wings.

Avis, "   ....general term, from which we get aviary.

Volucris, 'bird'..........bird because it flies.

Voltur, "   ....fr volitare, the bird that often flies, to get supplies.

Genus, 'manner'..........way of proceeding, argumentandi genus.

Consuetudo, 'manner'.....as custom or habit.

Modus,   "   ....mode or guide, modus operandi.

Ratio,   "   ....any way that may be thought of.

Ritus,   "   ....instinctive habit of animals.

Via,   "   ....a road, a sure method.

Facies, 'form'............surface view.

Figura, "   ....profile, from fingo, 'to shape.'

Forma, "   ....body outline; often used for shoe-last.

Species, "   ....form, but may be only imaginary, an ignis fatuus.

Specimen, "   ....a pattern by which the real may be known.

Acumen, 'trickery'........cunning that misleads, "makes the
worse appear the better reason."

Fraus,   "   ....damage by trickery.

Fraudatio,   "   ....the act of doing a wrong.

Dolus,   "   ....injury by deceit, as "one thing pre-
tended and another done," Dolus is
stronger than fraus.

Circumscriptio, 'trickery'..winding one up in a contract

Fallacia,   "   ..general term for any trick in word or
act that can deceive or mislead an-
other.

Concilium, 'council'.......the men who have come together for
counsel.

Consilium, 'counsel'......the deliberation of the council.

Consultatio, "   ......the action of deciding what is best.

Deliberatio, "   ......the action of weighing in the balances
the opinions expressed as to the best.

Onus, 'burden'.......... that which can be borne by man or
animal.

Moles,   "   ....heavy and shape'ess and oppressive.

Sarcina, "   ....but what we call a bundle, package,
luggage.

Desidia, 'indolence'.......as exhibited in sitting when work is to
be done.

Ignavia,   "   ....as shown by listlessness.

Inertia,   "   ....as an aversion to labor.

Pigritia,   "   ....
Pigrities,   as a disinclination to effort.

Segnitia,   "   ....as shown by always being behind, fol-
Segnities.   lowing, never leading.

Aura, 'favor'...........unre'iable favor.

Favor, "   ....helpfu'ness, encouragement from the
more powerful.

Gratia, 'favor'............grace, pleasure to both giver and re-
                         ceiver.

Studium, " ....from the lower toward the higher.

Venia,   " ....favor as pleasure to the receiver.

Alienatio, 'estrangement'..in feeling, but leading to actual sep-
                         aration.

Disjunctio,   "   ..in fact, and may be the result of
                         alienatio.

Dumetum, 'thicket'.......as denoting the place where thorn-
                         bushes grow.

Fruticetum,   " ....as denoting the place where shrubs or
                         other bushes grow.

Locus sentibus obsitus,
  'thicket' ....as a place planted with briers.

Cautio, 'caution'.........keeping away from danger. Cave
                         canem.

Provisio, " ....the action of seeing ahead, so as to
                         avoid.

Providentia, 'caution'.....the act which has been performed over
                         and over again by all the wise men
                         of the world from the most distant
                         ages.

Prudentia,   " .....often used for knowledge of any sub-
                         ject, a kind of sagacity.

Abundantia, 'abundance'...as of supplies whenever or wherever
                         found.

Copia,   " ...a collection already made.

Adulatio, 'flattery'........fawning as a dog.

Ambitio, " ....effort to gain favor.

Assentatio, 'flattery'......assenting to everything another says.

Blandimentum, 'flattery'...the thing presented as a bait.

Blanditia,   'flattery'... the abstract idea of flattery as expressed over and over in any part of the
world.

Obsequium,   "   ... following the beck and call of another.

Memoria, 'memory'....... the abstract and general term for the
faculty and for the remembrance of
anything past.

Recordatio,   "   ....:.... the action of bringing back what for
the time being we have not in mind;
our recollection.

Concordia, 'agreement'....: a heart to heart condition of agreement.

Consensio,   "   .... the action of being harmonious.

Consensus,   "   .... all separate acts of agreement taken
together.

Pax,   "   .... agreement between two parties to a
contract.

Unanimitas,   "   .... a state of oneness of mind about any
plan or work.

Urbs, 'city'.............. as one surrounded by a ring wall.

Municipium, 'city'........ a free city that has received the jus
civile Remanum.

Oppidum,   "   .... a fortified city, the fortification serving as a hindrance (ob) to the foot
(ped).

Civitas, 'state'............ as composed of citizens.

Republica, 'state'......... government, laws and property of a
country.

Prudentia, 'wisdom'....... seeing and preparing beforehand.

Sapientia,   "   .... good sound sense on all subjects, as
the essense of all experience.

Alumnus, 'son'...........forter-son, one cared for and educated as a son, but not a son by birth.

Filiolus, " ....a little son, but not grandson, as the Frenchman would think

Filius, " ....general term for son by birth, and always as legitimate.

Natus (gnatus) 'son'......a son by birth, but not necessarily legitimate.

Gener, " ......a son-in-law.

Privignus, " ......a step-son.

Liberi, 'children'........sons and daughters.

Aquila, 'standard'........the eagle of the legion.

Signum, " ....a national emblem, back of which were principles.

Vexillum, " ....a flag, large or small, fr. vehere, 'to carry,' was used by any one of the smaller commands.

Vulneratio, 'injury'.......as the action of giving wounds, general term.

Sauciatio, " ....as the action of wounding with a sharp instrument and so shedding blood.

Detrimentum, 'injury'.....an injury, if it be only a rub or a bruise.

Injuria, " ' .....whatever is contrary to ordinary right.

Incommodum, " .....as a mere inconvenience.

Damnum, " .....as a loss or a fine.

Malum, " .....as a common evil.

Vulnus, " .....as the general term, any considerable break to the body.

Noxia, " .....as any fault, offence or crime.

Bilis, 'anger'.............connected with a disordered liver.

Indignatio, 'anger'........as the expression of contempt for an unworthy action or villainous person.

Ira, "anger"........general term for any kind of rage.

Iracundia, " ....anger in waves from one who is naturally given to wrath.

Stomachus, " ....as the whole inner man breaking out in violence upon some object of wrath.

Ars, 'teaching'...........as a theory, *facultas* being used for the practice.

Disciplina, 'teaching'......as rather that which is to be learned.

Doctrina, " ......as that which is to be taught.

Eruditio, " ......as the action of bringing out of a rude state into a polished or polite condition.

Institutio, " ......as by arranging principles and using methods.

Praeceptum, " ......as a single lesson.

Praeceptio, " ......as by giving lessons in parts or by principles.

Professio, " ......public teaching.

Caespes, 'sod'............from *caedo*, sod and earth disunited.

Glaeba, " ....connected with *globus* and *glomus*, sod and earth united.

Lux, 'light'..............fr. *lugere*, as that which gives light or whiteness.

Lumen, 'light'............the most general term for every kind of light.

Vappa, 'wine'............sour wine.

Vinum, " ....any kind of wine,—the general term.

Merum, " ....not diluted with water.

Fructus, 'fruit'.......... fruit of the tree.

Frux, " .... fruit of the earth.

Pomum, " .... any one kind of fruit of a tree.

Advocatus, 'patron'....... one ca'led as an advocate or witness in any legal process.

Amator, " .... as one who loves and therefore helps sua sponte.

Consultor, " .... as one who gives advice.

Cultor, " .... as one who supports in every way his clients or friends.

Fautor, " .... as one who favors his friends.

Patronus, " .... as one who supports a body of clients.

Praeses, " .... as a protector of clients.

Clientela, 'patronage'...... as clientship, the relation of the weaker to the stronger.

Patrocinium, 'patronage'.. as a defence in a court of law

Praesidium, " .. as the protection of clients or as a guard to ward off enemies from the city.

Agricultura, 'farming'..... the business of farming.

Agricultio, " ..... the action of farming.

Asylum, 'refuge'........ from the Greek, and means 'freedom from the right of seizure.'

Perfug'um, " .... a place of perfect safety.

Praesidium, " .... as that which protects as would soldiers.

Portus, " .... as a harbour for ships endangered by storms.

Refugium, " .... as a place for retreat when overcome.

Receptaculum, 'refuge'.... as the place into which those who flee may be received.

Recessus,	'refuge'....	as a place in which one already lives because it has become his retreat.
Secessus,	"	as a p'ace of retirement from the heat of summer.
Ops,	'means'............	in any form or kind,—general term.
Copia,	"	collection of means of any kind.
Aes alienum,	'debt'........	because of being another person's money, which has been borrowed.
Res creditae,	"	will apply to any account for sundries may be money, may be goods, etc
Debitum,	"	any debt for anything.
Pecunia debita,	'debt'.....	the money that is due.
Co'latio,	'tax'............	special levy.
Onera,	"	regular yearly taxes.
Tributum,	'tax'..........	direct tax.
Vectigal,	"	indirect tax.
Bonum,	'advantage'......	as either material or moral.
Casus,	"	as an opportunity falling in one's way.
Commodum,	'advantage'	as a convenience in time, place or manner.
Commoditas,	"	as a state or condition of something.
Emolumentum,	"	as the result of effort.
Tempus,	"	as to seasonableness, the right time.
Fructus,	"	as to gain by growth
Lucrum,	"	as that which has been saved.
Potestas,	"	as an opportunity given to another person.
Utilitas,	"	as a state or condition for use.
Occasio,	"	as a favorable moment for action.
Opportunitas,	"	as a position reached, being always 'at the port.'

Dispendium, 'expense'.....as that which is gone from possession.
Impendium, " .....as that which inheres in a transaction.
Impensa, " .....as that which has been met in a transaction.
Sumptus, " .....as costs incident to one's life under any circumstances.

Modus, 'satiety'.........as a limit which has been reached.
Satietas, " ....as a state of appetite brought to a standstill.
Saturitas, " ....as a state of actual fulness.

Domus, 'home'.........as a dwelling-place for the family, including outbuildings and garden.
Domicilium, 'home'.......as a place for residence.
Sedes, " ....as a building.

Multitudo, 'people'........the people as a mass in general.
Plebs, " ....the common people, "so many of them."
Vulgus, " ....the people as the lower class.
Populus, " ....the people as free-born citizens.

Paedagogus, 'servant'.....one who cared for the boys on their way to and from school and at home.
Nutrix, " .....one who cared for the girls to and from the school and at home.
Audacia, 'boldness'.......natural boldness
Audentia, " ....assumed boldness.
Confidentia, 'boldness'.....boldness because of faith in self and others.

Exordium, 'beginning'.....of a speech.
Initium, ' " .....as an entry into any subject, work, or way.
Pr'ncipium, " .....as the first thing taken up.
Primordium, " .....as the real first in any work or way.

Inceptio,   'beginning'..... as the act of taking up a subject.

Inceptum,   "   ..... as the thing first undertaken.

Prima (nocte), 'beginning' as the first part of the night.

Primo (vespere)   "   . as the first part of the evening.

Ineunte (vere)   "   . at the very entering in of spring.

Novo (vere),   "   . as the new portion of spring.

Prima (fabula)   "   . as the first part of the story.

Ortus,   '   "   . as the rising of sun or moon or stars.

Elementa, 'beginnings'..... as the first things to be learned or con-
                                sidered.

Rudimenta,   "   ..... as the lowest and simplest things to be
                                tried

Incunabula,   "   ..... as the mere swaddling-clothes of any
                                subject.

Carmen, 'poem'.......... pure Latin from cano, 'sing,' a lyric
                                poem.

Poema,   "   .... Greek word for a lyric poem.

Pietas, 'piety'............ erga deum et parentes.

Religio,   "   .... religious feeling.

Sanctitas, 'piety'.......... holiness of life.

Sanctimonia, 'piety'....... virtuous sentiment.

Constantia, 'constancy'.... fixedness of purpose.

Patientia,   "   .... simple endurance of whatever is our
                                lot.

Perseverantia,   "   .... continuous activity in any undertaking.

Pervicacia,   "   .... innate persistency or obstinacy.

Perpetuitas,   "   .... uninterrupted continuance.

Fides,   "   .... as in keeping one's word.

Fidelitas,   "   .... as a condition or state of always doing
                                the right.

Continentia, 'continence'...as holding with a firm hand the reins
        on our appetites and passions.
Castitas,   " ...abstinence from sensual pleasure.
Castimonia,   " ...bodily or moral purity
Temperantia,   " ...in praetermittendis voluptatibus cer-
        nitur.—Cic.

Petulantia, 'capriciousness'. opp. pudor, as immodesty.
Inconstantia,   " . as fick'eness, the change being crafty.
Varietas,   " . as changeableness, the change coming
        often.
Infidelitas,   " . as not keeping one's word.
Levitas,   " . as lightheadedness, lightheartedness.
Mobilitas,   " . as capable of being moved by every
        wind of doctrine.
Mutabilitas,   " . as capab'e of being changed from one
        to another purpose.

Aetas, 'time'............any time of life.
Aevum, " ....often means one generation, and some-
        times even eternity.
Saeculum, 'time'..........an age, an indefinite period of time.
Tempus, " ....a fixed period of time.

Ultor, 'avenger'..........punisher of injuries.
Vindex, " ....protector against wrong.

Ora, 'shore'............steep land bordering on the sea, Fr.
        os, 'the mouth.'
Litus,   " ....land bordering on the sea, Fr. lino,
        'smear.'
Ripa,   " ....of a running stream.
Arena, " ....simply the sandy part.

Aegrotatio, 'sickness'......sickness now affecting the person.
Morbus,   " ......disease that is more or less chronic.

Negotium, 'thing'........ business of any kind, opp. of otium.
Res,   "   ....any object or subject in the universe.
Factum,   "   ....something already done, a fact.

Donum, 'gift'............as that which is intended to be a present.
Munus,   "   ....as that which has been promised.
Praemium, 'gift'..........as that which has been purchased by service.

Cruor, 'blood'............the heavier clotted blood.
Sanguis,   "   ....the lighter running blood.

Comes, 'companion'......traveling companion, but not under obligation to assist.
Conviva,   "   ......boon companion, as at a feast.
Socius,   "   ......as one sharing in business, a partner.
Sodalis,   "   '......as a member of the same club.

Argumentatio, 'proof'.....as something based upon facts.
Demonstratio,   "   .....as by the pointing out with the hand.
Documentum,   "   .....as that which has been taught or set forth by example.
Argumentum,   "   .....that which has cleared up a case.
Indicium,   "   .....as a discovery of what has been done.
Ratio,   "   .....as something grounded on reason.
Signum,   "   .....as a mere sign of what has been done or shall be done.
Specimen,   "   .....as a mark or example or token of what anything is.
Testimonium,   "   .....as a witness that has in itself the exhibition of what has been done.

Hereditas, 'patrimony'....anything that has come down to us from a former generation.

Patrimonium, 'patrimony'.. furniture and rich ware.

Praedia, "   .. what pertains to a farm as such.

Agitatio, 'movement'...... constant movement.

Motus, "   ...... any one movement.

Motio, "   ...... act of making any one movement.

Experientia, 'experience'... by anybody in anything at any time.

Experimentum, 'experience': in some one thing.

Periclitatio, "   . act of trying.

Usus, "   . everyday life.

Conversatio, "   . intercourse or employment.

Calamitas, 'destruction'.... as reverse in arms or failure in crops.

Caedes, "   .... as by cutting down with any instrument.

Clades, "   .... as by gladius, the sword.

Excid um, "   .... as falling from the very foundations.

Exitium, "   .... as the going out from life and hope.

Extinctio, "   .... as the snuffing out of a candle.

Interitus, "   .... as by separation of parts necessary for life.

Eversio, "   .... as the action of overturning from the foundation.

Pernicies, "   .... as complete death to person or things.

Dissolutio, "   .... as the going to atoms, disconnection of all parts

Ruina, "   .... as the falling of parts of a wall.

Strages, "   .... as by scattering to the winds.

Invidia, 'ill will'.......... which is shown by looking upon a person with evil eye.

Malevolentia, 'ill will'..... as always wishing evil to one hated.

Malignitas,	"	.....represented in a disposition to be evil and to do harm, and so always to be expected in the person.
Malitia,	"	.....as a state of mind, but not necessarily in more than one direction at a time.
Benevolentia,	'kindness'	...opp. to malevolentia, and hence wishing well.
Benignitas,	"	...opp. to malignitas, and so disposed to be and to do good.
Comitas,	"	...opp. to severitas, and so politeness courtesy.
Clementia,	"	...exhibited in mildness or mercy, but not necessarily from tenderness of heart.
Facilitas,	"	...disposition to be helpful and pleasant.
Humanitas,	"	...disposition to act as a human being
Indulgentia,	"	...a state of mind that, for the time being, forgets duties or dangers, and so yields even to the wrong.
Liberalitas,	"	...a disposition to be generous, noblehearted and true toward others.
Misericordia,	"	...exhibited in tenderness of heart and therefore mercy is the result of sympathy.

(8)

Pronouns.

(68)

Hic, 'this,' first personal pronoun representing what is near the speaker.

Iste, 'that,' second personal pronoun representing what is near the person addressed.

Ille, 'that,' third personal pronoun representing what is near the person spoken of or anything in the distance.

Is, 'that,' the person usually last pointed out, the usual antecedent of **qui.**

Idem, 'same,' the emphatic is, equal to is + dem.

Ipse, 'himself,' the emphatic reflexive se, equal to is + pse.

Alius, 'another,' as different from the speaker or person addressed. Hence, 'one of many.'

Alter, 'another,' one of two.

Ollus, 'that,' used as ille, to represent something distant.

Se, 'self,' we call it reflexive, but reflection is a secondary concept, and cannot be primary.

Egomet, 'I myself,' 'I by means of myself,' taking met as the ablative.

Qui, 'who,' a definite standard for is.

Quicunque, 'whosoever,' taken as an individual or 'whoso at any time.'

Quisquis, 'whosoever,' anybody including self.

Quis, 'any one,' an object merely conceived by the mind, but including self.

Quisnam, 'who pray,' a more lively and emphatic question.

Aliquis, 'some one' of any number of objects in actual existence, but excluding self.

Quisp'am, 'any one whosoever,' but in affirmative propositions,

Quisquam, 'any one whosoever,' contrasts with nemo, and includes self.

Ullus, 'any one whosoever,' contrasts with nullus.

Nonnullus, 'many a man,' and hence in the plural, 'not a few.'

Quidam, 'a certain one,' well-known and present to mind
Alteruter, 'each of two,' and so is really plural in meaning.
Quisque, 'every one,' distributively or relatively.

Unusquisque, 'each individual,' but including all without exception.
Uterque, 'each of two separately,' and then the idea of both.
Ambo, 'both together,' as acting jointly.
Quivis, 'any one whosoever,' of all the individual objects, so far as
          your wish extends
Quilibet, 'any one whosoever,' of all the individual objects, not
          according to your wish, but according to anybody's wish.
Utervis, 'which of the two separately' you may wish.
Uterlibet, 'which of the two separately' anybody may wish.

Nemo, 'no man,' ne + homo, 'not a human being,' always the ad-
          jective with national names.
Nemo non, 'every man' without exception.
Nullus, 'no one,' ne + ullus, 'not any individual,' Nullus scriptor,
          but nemo Romanus.
Nullus non, 'every one' without exception.
Nihil, 'nothing,' not a thread.
Nihil non, 'everything' without exception.
Neuter, 'neither of the two,' as the negative of uter.

Meus, 'mine,' beginning with M it denotes possession as a product
          or derivation or emanation of the ego.
Tuus, 'thine' unchanged as to stem is simply adjectival.
Noster, 'ours,' belonging to us-two as secondary to meus.
Vester, 'yours,' belonging to you-two as secondary to tuus.

Meopte, 'with my own,' as a contrast to other things not my own.
Meamet, 'with my own,' as a contrast to other things not my own.
Suopte, 'with his own,' as a contrast to other things not his own.
Suamet, 'with his own,' as a contrast to other things not his own.
Semet, 'self,' as a contrast of one's self with another.

Cujus, a, um, 'whose,' and following the gender of the noun.

Nostras, tis (gen.), 'of our nation,' following the gender of the noun.

Vestras, tis (gen.) 'of your nation,' following the gender of the noun.

Cujas, tis (gen.), 'of whose nation,' following the gender of the noun.

Qualiscunque, 'of any kind soever,' fr qualis + cum + que.

Qualislibet, 'of any kind anybody may like,' fr. qualis + libet.

Quantuscunque, 'of any size soever,' fr. quantus + cum + que.

Quantuslibet, 'of any size anybody may like, fr. quantus + libet.

Quantusvis, 'of any size you may wish,' fr. quantus + vis.

Quotcunque, 'any number whatsoever.'   (Both words being

Quotquot, 'whatever number'   (general in character.

Aliquantus, 'somewhat more,' the concept being that of increase in quantity.

Aliquot, 'some more,' the concept being that of increase in number.

Totidem, 'just so many,' an exact equality in number.

Quotus, 'as' the standard by which totus is measured.

Totus, 'so,' the thing to be measured by the standard quotus.

Quantulus, 'as little,' the standard of measurement.

Tantalus, 'so little,' the thing to be measured by the standard.

Quantuluscunque, 'as little as anything whatsoever.'

Aliquantulum, 'a very little more,' diminutive of aliquantus.

Tantundem, 'just so great,' and may run with quantum.

Tantidem, 'of so much value,' and may run with quanti.

FOURTH CHAPTER

STANDARDS AND THINGS TO BE MEASURED.

Those expressions which are introduced by the known representing the standard; and those introducing the unknown, and so yet to be understood and appreciated, representing the things to be measured.

STANDARDS AND THINGS TO BE MEASURED.

"Correlatives.," as called by the grammars.

Quantus—tantus, 'as—so,'—(referring to dimensions).
  The form beginning with qu always denoting the object whose measure is known and by which the object introduced by t is to become known.

Qualis—talis, 'as—so,'—(referring to characteristics).
  The form beginning with qu always denoting the object whose measure is known and by which the object introduced by t is to become known.

Quotus—totus, 'as—so.'
  The form beginning with qu always denoting the object whose measure is known and by which the object introduced by t is to become known.

Quot—tot,' 'as—so '—referring to number.
  The form beginning with qu always denoting the object whose measure is known and by which the object introduced by t is to become known.

Quam—tam, 'as—so,'—(referring to manner).
  . The form beginning with qu always denoting the object whose measure is known and by which the object introduced by t is to become known.

Quamquam—tamen, 'as—so,'—(referring to conditions).
  The form beginning with qu always denoting the object whose measure is known and by which the object introduced by t is to become known.

Quo—eo, 'as—so ·
Melius—melius, better,
Magis—magis, greater,
Minus—minus, less
  etc., etc., etc., etc.
  The form beginning with qu always denoting the object whose measure is known and by which the object introduced by t is to become known.

Quoties—toties, 'as—so,'—(in regard to times).
> The form beginning with qu always denoting the object
> whose measure is known and by which the object in-
> troduced by t is to become known.

Ut—sic, 'as—so,' rather a condition of exact parallelism, 'as I
said,'—'so it will be found.'

Sicut,   'so—as,' the two words combined. Ovid says sicut eram
Sicuti,   fugio, instead of ut eram, sic fugio.

All these words fall under Primary and Secondary Ideas; but
as they seem to require a little special notice, they are placed here
by themselves, in order to attract the student's attention to their
importance.

The words above listed follow the old rule of pedagogy, "that
the unknown must become known through the known which bears
some relation to the unknown."

This subject is of so much importance that we have treated it
in a work to itself under the title, "STANDARDS."

We will, however, here quote four pages from our book on
"Standards," in order to illustrate the thoughts so briefly treated
in this book:

The one peculiarity that must not be overlooked is the fact
that the part of the statement beginning with the guttural is the
one that is known or assumed to be known,—is the basis of measurement, and the one beginning with the dental is the one brought
up to be tested by the known or to be compared with it. Take for
example the following:

> 1. Tam sum misericors,
>   Quam vos; tam mitis quam qui lenissimus,—Sull. 87.

You are speaking to some person or persons supposed to know
how merciful they are; and hence you say, "I am as merciful as
you"; and more, "I am as mild as any one of the mildest." He says,
"Now, you know the person or some person who is 'very mild,' 'ex-
tremely mild.' Name that person, and I am 'equally mild.' "

2. **Quanto diutius considero,**
Tanto mihi res videtur obscurior,—DN. 1, 60.

'By as much the longer as I consider the matter,
'By so much the thing seems the more obscure to me.

Here my consideration is the thing known as to quantity and with my consideration already assumed I compare the obscurity, and the latter seems to measure up in quantity as a full parallel to my consideration.

3. **Qualis suavitas sermonum atque morum,**
Talis condimentum amicitiae.—Cic. de Am.

'As is the sweetness of conversation and character,
Such is the relish of friendship.'

Both parties are supposed to know 'the quality of sweetness in conversation and character," and so one who knows both the first and the last, says, "the relish of friendship is equal in quality to the first."

4. **Quot talenta habeam, 'As many** talents as I have,
Tot talenta dabo,—So many will I give.'

I will first ascertain "how many talents I have," then "so many talents will I give;" the one number shall equal the other.

5. **Cum dolore conficior,**
Tum etiam pudore.—Cic. Epis.

a. 'I am overcome both by grief and by shame.'

b. 'I am overcome not only by grief, but also by shame.'

c. **When I am overcome (so much) by shame, then also I am**
overcome (as much) (even as) by grief.'

You know how much I am overcome by grief: well, then, 'I am equally overcome by shame too, and you can measure my shame by the grief you know I feel."

6. **Quam** pirum volpes comest,
    Tam facile vinces,—Pl. Most. 559.

"As the fox eats the pear,
  So easily shall you conquer."

Now you know "how easily a fox eats a pear," then you can decide "how easily you shall conquer," for one is just as easy as the other: they are exactly parallel in the facility with which they can be done. Here we have the manner of the action.

7. **Quotiens** dicimus,
    Totiens de nobis judicatur,—Do. 1, 125.

"As often as we speak,
  Just so often is the judgment of us."

We know "how often we speak," and so by comparison we learn "how often people judge us;" judgment and speech run an equal race."

8. Quorum **quamdiu** mansit imitatio,
    Tamdiu genus illud dicendi vixit.

"The imitation of these persons remained as long,
  As that kind of speaking lived."

1. **Eum qui electus** (designatus) est
    Oportet sedem in senatu habere,

'He who has been elected
  Ought to have a seat in the Senate.'

Now, it is not "behooving" that just anybody should "have a seat in the senate," but the right to a seat depends on the fact of election: that is the one condition on which we say, eum oportet sedem in senatu habere.

2. **Homo qui hanc epistolam scripsit est stultus,**
   "The man who wrote this letter is a fool."

How do you know?   On what do you base your judgment,—Well, I know the man "who wrote this letter" and so do you, and nobody but a fool could write such a letter.   The letter establishes the folly.

3. **Nemo qui honester vivit potest vivere sine culpa.**
   No one who lives honorably can live without blame."

What you have called your "Restrictive Relative Clause" is the basis, on which the other part of the sentence rests.   In these degenerate days the man "who lives honorably" is marked by the mean and vile as one who should be cast down from his high estate, and hence the envious will seek to criminate, if by no other method than by falsehood.

4. **Cicero qui orationes ornatissimas facit**
   Est non solum orator, sed etiam scriptor,

"The Cicero who makes most beautiful orations
Is not only an orator, but also a litterateur."

4. **Cicero qui orationes ornatissimas facit,**
   Cum orator, tum scriptor cognitus est,

"The Cicero who makes most beautiful speeches,
Is recognized as equally a litterateur,—
As much a litterateur as (the known) an orator —

'When he is recognized as orator,
Then he is recognized as litterateur.'

Note the difference between these two statements In the first case he is both orator and litterateur, but his orations may surpass his other writings; whereas in the second case his other writings are recognized as equally good with his orations; but in both cases the estimate is based on the well-known orations.

5. Qui Dominum amat,—"He who loves his Master
    Ei serviet,—will serve him."

Our Savior said, "If you love me, keep my commandments." Now, if we are satisfied that our professions of love are sincere, then we know there will be no trouble about the service. The outside world, however, judges by our service whether we love our Master or not; but to ourselves the measure of love is the measure of cheerful service, and no one but ourselves can know whether we love the Master or not.

6. Cum ea ita sint,
    Tamen si obsides ab iis sibi dentur, sese cum iis pacem esse facturum, 'although,' etc.—Caes. Bel. Gal., Sec. 14.

Indirect narrative will always have the subjunctive, because that represents one person as speaking for another; and although the writer may know, still as not speaking for himself he must appear as assuming that some one else does know that of which he speaks or writes.

IN OUR INDEX

We have put all Nouns, Adjectives, etc , in the Nominative case
and Singular number and all our Verbs in the Present Infinitive
and Active Voice.

LATIN INDEX.

A

ENGLISH INDEX.

(158)